THE RIVER NUTS

Other Books by Avrel Seale

The Hull, the Sail, and the Rudder:
    A Search for the Boundaries of the Body, Mind and Soul

The Secret of Suranesh

True Freedom and the Wisdom of Virtue

The Tree: A Spiritual Proposition, and Selected Essays

Dude: A Generation X Memoir

The Grand Merengue

Staggering: Life and Death on the Texas Frontier at Staggers Point

Monster Hike: A 100-Mile Inquiry into the Sasquatch Mystery

With One Hand Tied behind My Brain: A Memoir of Life after Stroke

THE RIVER NUTS

DOWN THE NUECES WITH ONE STROKE

AVREL SEALE

Afterword by **WADE WALKER**
Illustrations by **DAVID McLEOD**

FORT WORTH, TEXAS

Copyright © 2023 by Avrel Seale

Library of Congress Cataloging-in-Publication Data

Names: Seale, Avrel, 1967– author.
Title: The River Nuts : down the Nueces with one stroke / Avrel Seale.
Other titles: Down the Nueces with one stroke
Description: Fort Worth : TCU Press, [2023] | Summary: "Writer and weekend outdoorsman Avrel Seale had always dreamed of boating down a river to the sea, but he had never found the right boat, the right river, or the right opportunity. Then, at age fifty, he suffered a massive brain hemorrhage, depriving him of the use of one arm, among other things. But, as he writes, "dreams are stubborn things," and less than two years after his stroke, he was again mulling such a trip. With the recruitment of a lifelong friend and the purchase of a two-person pedal kayak, he set out to journey down the Nueces River in South Texas to the Gulf of Mexico. The resulting memoir is a study in perseverance and ingenious problem-solving set against the backdrop of an under-appreciated river. Seale must overcome numerous physical, mechanical, and logistical challenges to even get to the starting line. Then, he and Wade Walker set out to descend the Nueces, once considered by Mexico to be its border with the United States. Today, the Nueces (Spanish for "nuts") is a twisting ribbon of prehistoric beauty, lush and wild, secretly flowing just out of view of the cotton towns, truck stops, and wind farms that line the highways of Texas's coastal plains"— Provided by publisher.
Identifiers: LCCN 2023007681 (print) | LCCN 2023007682 (ebook) | ISBN 9780875658520 (paperback) | ISBN 9780875658599 (ebook)
Subjects: LCSH: Seale, Avrel, 1967—Travel—Texas—Nueces River. | Journalists—Texas—Austin—Biography. | Outdoorsmen—Texas—Austin—Biography. | Cerebrovascular disease—Patients—Texas—Austin—Biography. | Kayaking for people with disabilities—Texas—Nueces River. | Nueces River (Tex.)—Description and travel. | LCGFT: Travel writing.
Classification: LCC F392.N82 S43 2023 (print) | LCC F392.N82 (ebook) | DDC 917.64/11—dc23/eng/20230419
LC record available at https://lccn.loc.gov/2023007681
LC ebook record available at https://lccn.loc.gov/2023007682

TCU Box 298300
Fort Worth, Texas 76129

Design by Julie Rushing

CONTENTS

PART I

ONE	WAYS OF GOING UPON THE WATER	3
TWO	ONE WAY LEFT	10
THREE	SOMETHING IN THE NOTHING	14
FOUR	THE VIRGIN VOYAGE OF THE COMET	21
FIVE	ROLLING IN THE DEEP	30
SIX	THE SHADE TREE MECHANIC	37
SEVEN	THE SHAKEDOWN	41
EIGHT	THE LAYING ON OF EYES	49
NINE	SLOW BOAT FROM CHINA	55
TEN	THE FINAL COUNTDOWN	61

PART II

ELEVEN	ÁNDA!	67
TWELVE	GARLAND	73
THIRTEEN	A DAMMED SHAME	87
FOURTEEN	JUST WANNA GET DOWN	96
FIFTEEN	SCRAPING BY	103
SIXTEEN	THE RIGHTS OF MAN	109
SEVENTEEN	PALMETTOS AND PACHANGAS	113
EIGHTEEN	BRACKISH	127
NINETEEN	THE OLD MEN . . .	131
TWENTY	. . . AND THE SEA	136

AFTERWORD BY WADE WALKER 147
ACKNOWLEDGMENTS 153

For Wade Walker

*If at any time in the following pages
I slip up and say "we" did something,
what I really meant to say was
Wade did that thing.*

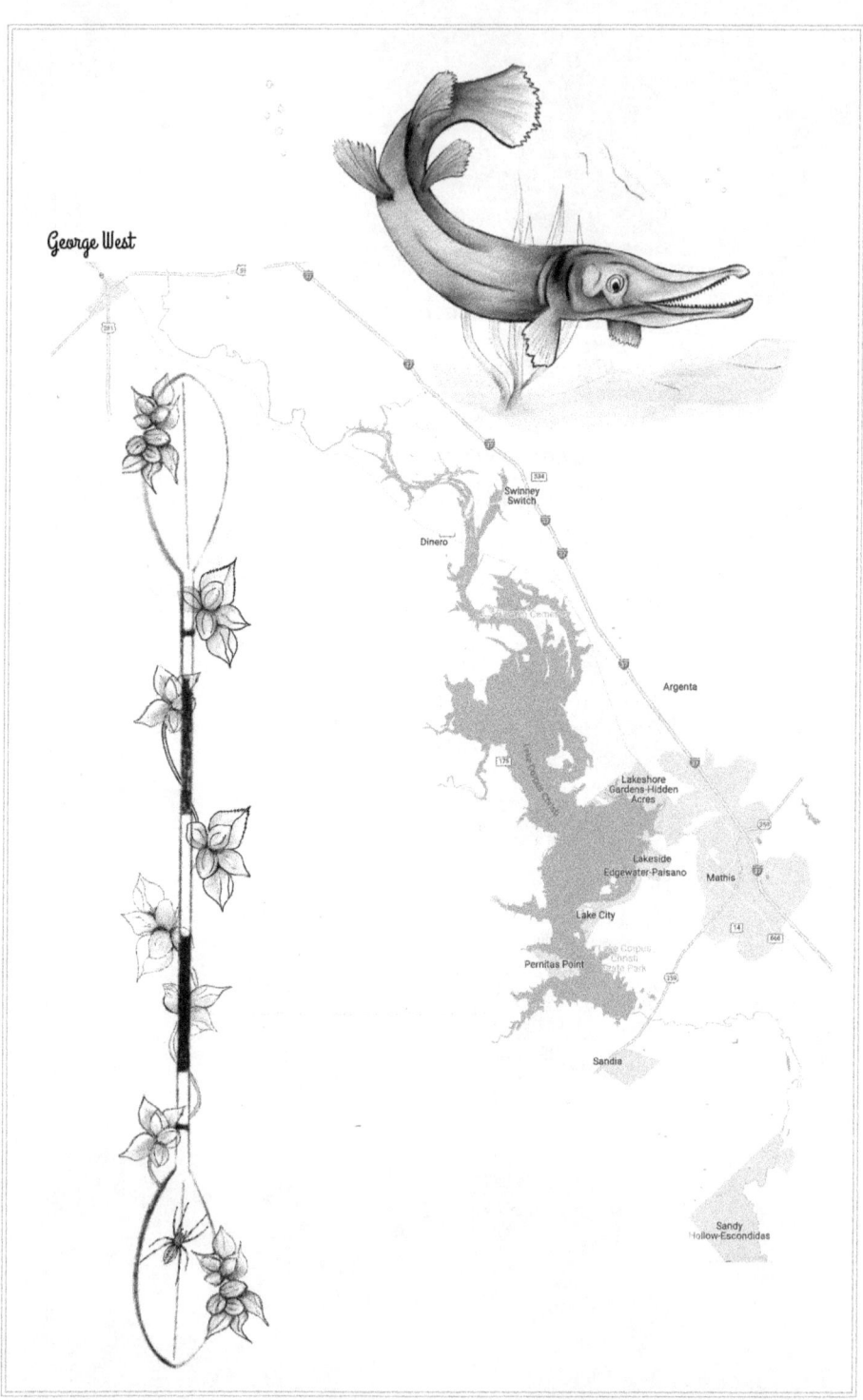

The Lower Nueces River

*"Adventure is just the word
for a venture with adversity."*

**—PARK RANGER TO ME
YOSEMITE NATIONAL PARK, 2019**

PART I

ONE

WAYS OF GOING UPON THE WATER

"There is only one thing that makes a dream impossible to achieve: the fear of failure." —**PAULO COELHO**

"What a crock." —**AVREL SEALE**

THE WHITE THREE-RING BINDER sat on a paper placemat at the table near the sugar packets and salt and pepper shakers. I had arrived at J&J's a few minutes early, as was my habit, and at eight a.m., Wade walked through the door. He had the same smile on his face that either of us had when we hadn't seen each other in a while, a smile of anticipation that the other one was about to do or say something crude and funny. Semi-rimless glasses framed his smiling eyes. With a lean runner's physique, close-cropped salt-and-pepper hair tamed with a dab of product, and a mustache and beard trimmed just longer than stubble, he was aging well.

But meeting for breakfast at eight on a Saturday morning was a sure sign that we were getting old, and could no longer sleep in even if we wanted to. I suppose we had joined the ranks of old men across America who gather for breakfast every Saturday morning at Dairy Queens, sitting for hours and drinking coffee in John Deere hats, sitting at the tables instead of the booths, which were much harder to get into and out of.

THE RIVER NUTS

Wade Walker and I were sixteen when we met and became buddies, and on a few occasions back in high school, when one set of parents or the other were out of pocket, we would not even have gotten home from the Mexican border city of Reynosa by this hour of the day. Anymore, the only reason I was ever up late on a Friday night was to pick up my middle son from his high school at eleven-whatever p.m. once the band buses had returned after a game. Though Wade was a few months younger than me, he had gotten a somewhat earlier start in the fathering business, and his youngest of three was now a college freshman.

It was November 2019, and I had asked Wade to meet me for breakfast and given him a vague warning that I was going to pitch him a crazy idea. As we waited for the number to be called that meant our pancakes, bacon, and eggs were ready, I reached for the white three-ring binder. "Okay, dude, here's the deal."

―――

I think it was something I always had wanted to do—go under my own power down a river to the sea. At its core, I think, were both the idea and the sensation of freedom. Whereas in the middle of the 1800s, a person with a wild hair could have walked overland from almost any point to any other point, barbed wire and trigger-happy landowners had put a stop to that sort of freedom more than a century ago, to the righteous chagrin of Woody Guthrie and other free spirits. Enough generations have passed between then and now that most folks seem to have forgotten that we even *could* roam, and that perhaps as a species, once in a while, we needed to roam, to see new things, unexpected things.

Living in a world so thoroughly carved up and sold off, there were only two ways I had discovered for the common man still to really experience freedom in nature the way it once must have been everywhere. One way was hiking through a national forest; this was something I had done a few years earlier. The other way was traveling on a river, which,

WAYS OF GOING UPON THE WATER

Wade (*standing*) and me (*sitting*), guiding the Sterilite raft past a "sweeper" on the Colorado River.

although usually flanked by private property, nevertheless was itself considered public property, and by Texas law one was allowed to camp along its banks when enroute (of which more later).

The archetype of a free Huck Finn was powerful, and perhaps twenty years earlier I had started to really entertain notions of a river trip and calculate if it was something I actually could pull off.

I had thought first of a canoe trip. With visions of Lewis and Clark tap-dancing in my subconscious, I imagined taking a few weeks and perhaps floating down the Colorado from Austin to the Gulf of Mexico, camping all along the way. This desire was stoked by Nathaniel Stone's remarkable book *On the Water: Discovering America in a Row Boat*, in which Stone, after discovering that, but for a twenty-mile portage, the entire eastern third of the United States could be circumnavigated by boat, did just that, alone.

For a time, I entertained going full Huck Finn and even built a raft. It was not a primitive raft of lashed logs or lumber. But neither was it a modern inflatable raft—those bouncy castles of yellow or red that would not have been recognizable to river-going folk of any previous age. Rather,

Breaking camp on an island between Austin and Bastrop on the same raft trip.

when assembled, it was an eight-foot by sixteen-foot platform built of plywood that, at the water's edge, got bolted onto forty plastic Sterilite storage bins. It was highly unconventional and labor-intensive to build. I took it out three times: first to a nearby lake for its virgin voyage. Next to Lady Bird Lake (the section of Texas's Colorado River that runs through downtown Austin). Finally, I had talked Wade into bringing Jackson, his youngest, and joining my boys and me on a one-night trip down the Colorado below Austin to Bastrop. It was a great adventure. We camped on an island in the river, and we proved that six people could go fifteen miles down a river floating on Sterilite storage bins and live to tell about it.

———

Then, at age fifty and perfectly healthy, I had a stroke.

It was not a "ministroke," the kind people bounce back from in a month or two, but a doozie: a 4.7 centimeter hemorrhage caused by a malformed artery that ruptured one afternoon out of the blue when I was at work. It required emergency brain surgery that likely saved my life. I spent five weeks in hospitals and another five weeks in an inpatient neuro-rehabilitation facility.

The stroke had flattened me. But, by the grace of God and the patient work of lots and lots of therapists, I recovered the ability to walk and to do many of the things I had loved doing for the first fifty years of life, albeit with significant struggle. One thing that to this day has not returned is the function of my right hand, and yes, I was right-handed. Maybe I still am right-handed, but if a tree falls in the forest and no brain cells are there to hear it, does it make a sound? At any rate, as you might imagine, losing the use of a hand, let alone one's dominant hand, forecloses all sorts of activities. My right leg still worked well enough that, with the help of a brace that prevented me from turning my ankle with every step, I could get from point A to point B. But it wasn't pretty. I now walked with a significant limp and had to actively think about keeping my balance when on the move, and only with great struggle could I do things like squat, sit on the ground, roll over, and get off the ground.

But dreams are stubborn things, and within two years of the stroke, the thought of camping down a river to the sea reared its head above the water's surface of my injured brain again. As a goal for someone with my level of disability, it resided somewhere on a spectrum between audacious and bat-shit crazy, but I couldn't shake it. To surrender this dream to the stroke, as a completely sane, prudent person probably would have, was something I simply wasn't willing to do. Not pursuing the dream might prolong my life, but would that life have felt like really living?

The first thing you might wonder about a stroke survivor planning a river trip is whether said survivor can swim. I had, with the help of my Red Cross-certified lifeguard son, first braved the neighborhood pool a few months after returning home from my hospitalization. The pool had a "beach entrance," slowly sloping from one inch to a depth of about four feet. When I reached swimming depth, with Andrew at my elbow, I slowly pitched forward and, knowing that I could stand up if I needed to, tried a few strokes. I tried to swim a normal freestyle stroke but went in a circle, of course, as I could only paddle with one arm and kick with one leg.

Trying a little bit of everything, I decided to see what backstroking felt like, so I turned on my back, reached as far overhead as I could, and pulled my arm straight down behind me. It was far from perfect, even far from good, but I could float, I could breathe at will, and I could move from one side of the pool to the other, usually in a route as circuitous as a relentlessly meandering river. After three or four trips to the pool, I even managed to lane swim twenty-five yards down and back, only occasionally plowing into a lane line, thrashing to keep my head above water, or coughing violently when I failed. Again, it was nothing pretty, and drew a lot of concerned stares from the lifeguards on duty, but it was enough to convince me that if I did fall out of a boat, I could get to the riverbank.

I thought again of the raft. After all, I had invested so much time and work in it. But it was just too much for me to handle after the stroke. The lifting, the bolting of hardware all with my non-dominant hand, the freakshow of transporting it to water, the near impossibility of portage—it was challenging when I was physically whole, but now it was simply too much. When I finally realized that I could never use it again, I could not even convince anyone to take the thousand-dollar vessel off my hands "free to a good home" due to its unconventionality. The plywood platforms, the hardware—it all still sits under my crude boathouse gathering cobwebs as the forty Sterilite bins, in tall nested stacks, grow ever more brittle baking and freezing with each passing cycle of seasons.

If I was going to do this, I needed to think light, think small, get back to basics. My mind returned to the original fantasy, to a canoe.

On a Boy Scout campout to Lake Georgetown just north of Austin, I sat on the front seat of one of the eight canoes we had rented and did my best to grip the paddle handle with Pancho, my nickname for my neurologically deaf right hand, and paddle on my left. But each time I dipped my paddle into the water, it would only create drag and nearly get pulled out of my grip. Perhaps this was because Andrew, my seventeen-year-old son sitting in the back, had paddled the Minnesota boundary waters the previous summer and knew how to get a canoe moving better than most. But I knew within five minutes that this was not to be. Just sitting in the canoe was extremely uncomfortable. My nearly paralyzed right arm put paddling somewhere between ineffective and impossible. And what little paddling I could do was only on my left. Significant paddling—let alone paddling all day for a week or more—was out of the question.

Raft, no. Canoe, no. There was exactly one option left.

TWO

ONE WAY LEFT

"Just-in-time: denoting a manufacturing system in which materials or components are delivered immediately before they are required..." —**OXFORD DICTIONARY**

THERE WAS ONE CLASS OF VESSEL remaining that used human power, and that was a form of kayak driven by pedals that turned a propeller under the boat. These had been created so that anglers could maneuver their kayaks in the water without having to put down their rods to paddle. But they also allowed people with upper-body disabilities to operate a boat. A kayak—a sit-on-top kayak, not the traditional sit-inside kind—would alleviate the discomfort of the low-bench seating arrangement of a canoe and put the paddler—er, pedaler—into a recumbent position that I thought I could manage.

Traditional kayaks were built by the indigenous people of the North American arctic at least four thousand years ago to hunt seals. Some years later, in 1971 to be exact, Tim Niemeyer carved up his surfboard with one compartment to hold a seat and another for his skin-diving gear. The sit-on-top kayak was thus born, probably to "Brown Sugar" or "Riders on the Storm" playing on a garage radio. His idea roughly coincided with the appearance of rotomolded plastic kayaks, the first of which was made in 1973. Niemeyer's concept caught on during the 1980s, and by the mid-nineties, virtually every kayak manufacturer produced a "sit-on-top" or "ocean" model.

ONE WAY LEFT

These boats bear little resemblance to true kayaks, whether in their appearance, their physics, or the skills required to operate them. Sitting on top means a higher center of gravity, which necessitates a wider, flatter hull, which in turn makes the boats slower and less maneuverable. On the upside, you're not sitting inside a tube that's half submerged. You're sitting about four inches above the water line, and you're not inside anything.

So as I say, calling these boats "kayaks" is a little like calling a dog a "cat" because it has four legs, fur, and a tail. Ocean, or sit-on-top, kayaks share more DNA with the surfboard from which they evolved than the kayak. The only similarity left between these boats and actual kayaks is that the operators of each use double-bladed paddles to power and maneuver them.

But of course, that similarity can be taken away, too, which in my case was the whole point. The first pedal kayaks appeared in 1997, when Hobie, well known for making small sailboats, introduced its Mirage drive, a fish-inspired design in which the pedaler operates two scissor-like fins beneath the boat. In 2008, Native Watercraft introduced its own system in which pedals drove a propeller. With the addition of pedals, these boats resemble a cross between a canoe and a recumbent bicycle.

Therefore, this particular kind of boat had existed only about a decade when I concluded it was my last option for making a river trip. In the four-thousand-year sweep of kayak history, it had come along in the nick of time. Call it whatever you want—I was glad the Inuits, and Tim Niemeyer, and Hobie, and Native Watercraft had come up with this way of going upon the water.

~~~~~~

I was adventurous, but by no means did I have a death wish. If I was to do this at all, it would need to be with someone else. I had undertaken a similarly ambitious project before my stroke, doing a hundred-mile hike across Sam Houston National Forest. I had wanted to do that with someone else, but when I had no takers, I cowboyed up and did it by my lonesome.[1]

But my situation was now profoundly different. I was a fool, no doubt, but I was not fool enough to think I could do this alone. I had a wife and three boys to come home to, and wherever I went and whatever I did, I certainly wanted to come home.

So I started shopping for a tandem pedal kayak, a sort of aquatic bicycle built for two. I found only two models. One was a Hobie and cost more than three thousand dollars. The other was built by a lesser-known outfit named Outer Banks Kayaks,[2] had propeller drives, and was about two thousand dollars.

As a state employee, and as an author who had sold tens upon tens of books, two grand was a big investment for me, and so before I took the plunge I wanted to know I had a partner in crime. That's why I invited Wade to breakfast that November morning with a printout showing the boat in that white three-ring binder and a loose plan of what I wanted to do with it.

"I'm in," he said.

"It's going to be hard," I warned him. "There will be times you'll wish like hell you hadn't agreed to this, and times you'll probably hate my guts."

"It'll build character," he said.

Yes, I thought, it will. He gets it.

I wanted to try it out before buying one, naturally. As I mentioned, I had thought I could maneuver a canoe, but five minutes actually sitting in one had convinced me otherwise. So I tried to find a pedal kayak I

---

1. This adventure is chronicled in the book *Monster Hike: A 100-Mile Inquiry to the Sasquatch Mystery*.
2. Not actual name.

could rent, but when I explained to anyone at a kayak rental place on the phone what I was looking for, all they said was, "Yeah, I think those are only for fishing. Anyway, we don't have any." In retrospect, it probably was a good thing that I could not find one to try out because, for reasons you will soon understand, I wouldn't have been able to operate one that wasn't modified, and so might have given up on the whole project.

For now though, ignorance was bliss, and I trusted that whatever difficulties I might encounter with the boat could be overcome if it was mine to tinker with. For about three weeks I had left a tab in my browser open on the Outer Banks 14TPK—that's for fourteen-foot tandem pedal kayak—in the gray camo pattern.

At last, a Black Friday discount of thirty percent pushed me over the edge. I entered my credit card number, its expiration date and security code, drew a deep breath, and clicked "Purchase."

THREE

SOMETHING IN THE NOTHING

"What makes the desert beautiful is that somewhere it hides a well." —ANTOINE DE SAINT-EXUPERY

"No, that's not really it." —AVREL SEALE

WHILE I WAITED FOR THE BOAT, I mulled which river would be best to attempt.

I was by this time in my life a habitual memoirist, having written four books in that genre, and must admit I was thinking in book-marketing terms. And as I was committed to pedaling a Texas river, I first considered the Trinity. I thought going source to sea on a river that passed through both the Dallas and Houston metropolitan areas would create splendid promotional opportunities. Then I came across the mileage. The Trinity is seven hundred fifty miles long. At a generous twenty miles a day, that would take more than a month, and passing through multiple large lakes would make it even slower. For two people with full-time jobs and kids, that dog would not, under any circumstances, hunt.

The Colorado River was the closest to home, as it ran right through downtown Austin, but it was also too long. Same for the Brazos, which John Graves had already squeezed dry with his 1959 classic memoir *Goodbye to a River*. (By the way, it is still there.)

SOMETHING IN THE NOTHING

For a few days, I studied the San Antonio River. It certainly had good name recognition and loads of rich history, but following it downstream on Google Maps' satellite view revealed that it basically shriveled up to something only occasionally navigable before it reached the Gulf.

The Rio Grande had A-list name recognition and was ever-pregnant with current events and political and philosophical messages. What's more, it offered a solid nostalgic hook as the river of my boyhood and Wade's, as we had grown up ten miles from its banks in McAllen. But there were plenty of cons too: It was incredibly dangerous. Mexican drug cartels owned the river far more than ever before and might pick us off from a bluff with an AR just for sport. As a subject for a travel memoir, it had been covered before many times, and to an extent I could not hope to compete with. Moreover, despite its name (Large River), it was so pitiful for much of its length, so siphoned off to irrigate a vast region that spanned two countries, that, depending on rainfall, it sometimes did not even reach the Gulf. How disappointing would *that* be at journey's end? Finally, we couldn't camp river-right without illegally entering a foreign country, which would make for interesting reading but, again, only if I lived to tell the tale.

I searched the map again, and at last my eyes fell upon a river I had crossed probably two hundred times going between my adopted home of Austin and my hometown of McAllen but had never given much thought to: the Nueces.

The Nueces bisected a region my friends and I long had called The Nothing. *Mad Max 3: Beyond Thunderdome* had come out my senior year of high school and so was still fresh in our minds as we began making trips as college freshmen back and forth between McAllen and Central Texas. In *Mad Max*, The Nothing was a vast expanse of desert in The Wasteland of post-apocalyptic Australia.

Our Nothing at that age was a wasteland to be gotten through in order to get home. At the north edge sat San Antonio, America's seventh largest city. At the south edge was the Rio Grande Valley, delineated by palm trees like an actual oasis, as if to drive home the emptiness of The Nothing to its north. At the end of the four-hour drive from San Antonio—quiet, flat, and so straight a road you could have tied your steering wheel to your blinker with a length of string and made it just fine—the first palm trees north of Edinburg felt like coming into Cairo from the Sahara, or so I supposed. "The Valley," as it's known to Texans despite the absence of any surrounding mountains, felt like a thriving tropical metropolis of culture and commerce by comparison.

Hour after hour, we sped due south upon a sea of sagebrush and mesquite, punctuated about every forty-five minutes by small towns we knew nothing of except on which side of the highway their Dairy Queens were situated: Three Rivers (left), George West (right), Alice (left), Premont (right), Falfurrias (right), (border patrol checkpoint), San Manuel (no Dairy Queen, but a chorizo factory with giant pig painted on it off the road on the left). This was our version of "flyover country," and we slowed down only enough to avoid a ticket—and were not always successful at that.

The widely spaced small towns were in various states of depopulated poverty and existed almost entirely at the whim of surrounding oil and gas fields, always seeming like the remnants of some better time just past. Now a junkyard. Now a boarded-up filling station with a stray dog wandering by. Now a low-slung motel with a peeling, decades-old sign proudly advertising that every room had air conditioning and a color TV.

Take away everything that had ever been built to service the oil and gas industry, and what remained would have been crossroads with a flashing yellow light, those roads connecting ranching operations and far-flung deer leases.

The Nothing is an unkind name for any place, I grant you. Saudi Arabia's "Empty Quarter" could probably relate, as could the entire nation of Mongolia. But we were young and unobservant and appreciated only bright lights and big cities. When we did appreciate nature, it was the beach or the mountains, if we had ever seen any. It certainly wasn't this—what naturalists call "the Tamaulipan Thornscrub."

But with age can come a sophistication of observation, and you begin to appreciate your flyover country. You begin to understand that all places have their charms; they're just not in the obvious places, where you've been looking for them. Your eyes stop searching in vain for postcard vistas like mountains and waterfalls, and instead your focus moves closer, and you start to notice the subtleties—the intricacies of a huisache tree's compound leaf, the way morning light shows through a jackrabbit's translucent ears, provided you can spot the jackrabbit. You begin to realize there is something in The Nothing.

There is a brutal beauty in this land. Arid and thorny and not for the sissies of any species, including our own. For untold millenia the land resisted settlement of any kind. The Homo sapiens who dared to live here subsisted on a razor-thin margin of carbohydrates and protein: cactus fruit, roots, mesquite beans, lizards, and the occasional windfall of a deer or javelina. They remained so occupied with squeezing sustenance out of the stingy land that they could not develop a culture that we can see beyond the arrival of Spanish missionaries and militia. Scholars lump them together under the name Coahuiltecans, but in reality, as of the time of European contact, they existed as dozens of tiny nomadic bands living hand-to-mouth with Stone Age technology. They must have been both ingenious and as tough as nails.

Though it eventually drains The Nothing, the Nueces rises in the Texas Hill Country and winds its way for a little more than three hundred miles, emptying into the Nueces Bay, which connects to Corpus Christi Bay on the Gulf of Mexico, about halfway between Galveston to the northeast and South Padre Island downcoast. I had come to it by a process of elimination, but it had possibilities.

And it had history. It was the first river in modern Texas to appear on a European map, though by a different name, Rio Escondido. For the next three hundred years it was crisscrossed by Spanish conquistadors, while the aforementioned native Coahuiltecan people were pushed to the brink of extinction by Apache and Comanche aggression and finally absorbed into Spanish culture when they sought refuge from other Indian tribes at Spanish missions. In the 1840s, Mexico considered

The Padron Real, 1527, drawn by Portuguese cartographer Diogo Ribeiro and considered the first scientific world map. The Nueces River is labeled the Río Escondido, or "Hidden River," because its mouth was obscured by what we call North Padre Island or Mustang Island. Original in the Herzogin Anna Amalia Bibliothek, Weimar, Germany.

the Nueces its border with the United States. The United States begged to differ, and the war that resulted drastically redrew the map of both nations. I knew none of this when we dubbed the region drained by this river The Nothing.

If you search internet videos for "Nueces" and "kayaking," "paddling," or anything similar, four out of five hits will show the first third of the river, the Hill Country section. Here, running through scenic canyons, the water is crystal clear and the surroundings gorgeous. It was in this section, somewhere in the vicinity of Carrizo Springs, that Spanish explorer Alonso De León and chaplain Damián Massanet crossed the river in 1689, bushwhacking their way from Coahuila, south of the Rio Grande, across Texas to the northeast in their fourth attempt to find and destroy France's precarious toehold in Texas, the La Salle settlement. When they hit the Nueces in what is now Dimmit or Zavala County, where it passes only about thirty miles from the Rio Grande, they named it Río de las Nueces, "River of the Nuts," for the plentiful pecan trees that grew on that stretch.

But the very thing that made the Hill Country section of the Nueces so classically beautiful also made it impossible for me: limestone. The limestone giveth—clear water, scenic cliffs, babbling rapids; and the limestone taketh away—a rocky riverbed that constantly turned shallow was impossible for a propeller-driven boat. That stretch called for a different type of vessel—and a much better swimmer.

For several months I considered putting in near Cotulla and trying to do the lower two-thirds of the river. Cotulla sits on I-35 midway between San Antonio and Laredo and has a legitimate claim in American history as the true birthplace of the Great Society. It was there that LBJ went to teach after college in San Marcos, and the extreme poverty he witnessed there among the Mexican American families whose children he taught (can you imagine Lyndon Johnson being your grade school teacher?) set him on a course to become a social-welfare president second only to Franklin Roosevelt.

THE RIVER NUTS

But close examination of satellite imagery of the middle third of the river—the section between I-35 and US 281—cast serious doubt on its status as a navigable stream. Upstream from Cotulla a click or two was Crystal City, which by its name sounded like a delightful spot from which to embark. The Google satellite image showed a river snaking its way through the region, but when I clicked on a bridge that crossed that river, and zoomed all the way down to Street View, a funny thing happened. The river went away completely. Where a Google intern had apparently colored the stream bed a refreshing shade of teal to show the course of the river, Street View showed naught but a bone-dry ditch, one filled with high weeds, bushes, and full-grown trees growing in its deepest parts.

It was then that I decided to make my goal roughly the final third of the Nueces, from US 281, which runs from San Antonio to the Rio Grande Valley, to Corpus Christi on the Nueces Bay. It wasn't as adventurous as camping down the Mississippi source to sea. It wasn't as ambitious as rowing around the eastern third of the United States. But for two fifty-something kayaking novices—one of whom had significant brain damage, and the other who had suffered a stroke *(badoom ching!)*—it seemed like a sufficiently audacious goal. Adventure is entirely relative to ability.

FOUR

THE VIRGIN VOYAGE OF THE COMET

"My general plan is good, though in the detail there may be faults." —**ADAM WEISHAUPT, GERMAN PHILOSOPHER (1748-1830)**

A FEW DAYS PASSED, and I had not seen any movement on the shipping website, so I began wondering where my new kayak was coming from. A search for Outer Banks Kayaks showed its headquarters was not in Raleigh or Wilmington or Cape Hatteras, but in New Jersey. But when I entered my order number, the site said my boat was being shipped from Rancho Dominguez, California.

Not familiar with Rancho Dominguez, I searched on the name and learned that it was a district inside of Compton, that southern California hamlet infamous for gang violence. Between New Jersey and Compton, I was pretty sure someone had gotten their ass capped in the making and delivery of my kayak, another sad loss in the decades-long East Coast/West Coast rap feud. Before it even arrived, I had dubbed the vessel *The Compton Comet*. It was mainly for the alliteration, but also worked visually in terms of its icy gray camo pattern.

It arrived on December 19, just after dark, in a large freight truck backing carefully into our cul-de-sac. With the prior blessing of my wife, Kirstin, I asked the driver and his wingman to please go ahead and walk it up the sidewalk and just set it in our front room. This request was met with a chuckle and a tactful refusal, amplified by a side note that never before had someone asked them to put a boat inside a house. They set the kayak, wrapped in cardboard and clear plastic, and two additional large boxes containing the steel propeller drives, in the yard, and I signed for it with my nondominant left-handed chicken scratch.

Cameron, my fifteen-year-old son, and Micky, a family friend, turned it on its side, fed it through the front door, then pivoted it into the front room. At fourteen feet long, it cut an impressive profile and thoroughly dominated the space. The next thirty minutes was a riot of plastic straps, plastic wrap, bubble wrap, corrugated cardboard, and hardware baggies. Then we attacked the drive boxes, hastily and joyfully screwing them all together with the provided allen wrenches and setting the drives and the seats in place. For me, Christmas had come early.

The next morning I got the boys to help me raise the boat up on two sawhorses to get a closer look and so I would not need to stoop to inspect or fidget with it.

This will not be too technical, but as our tale unfolds, the gentle reader will appreciate having a basic knowledge of this craft.

Like all such sit-on-top kayaks, this one was rotomolded in two halves, top and bottom, that then were welded, or melted, together to form a hollow hull. There were three ways to get into the hull to store things: a large oval hatch on top of the nose, or bow, and two circular hatches about five inches across under each seat, each with a cover that screwed on for a tight seal. Inside, each of these hatches held a red polyester baggie to hold small items, without which things would simply slide around throughout the hull and be impossible to reach. The boat was molded to have two shallow cockpits, one for each person. Inside each cockpit were six holes about two inches wide that ran straight through to the bottom of the boat to allow water to flow out of the cockpit if it was higher than the waterline. Matching up and

The author with son Cameron the night of the kayak's arrival.

welding perfectly the two halves of each of these twelve "scupper holes" is a critical step in the manufacturing process that seals the hull. And each scupper hole has its own rubber plug to keep water out when the boat is underway—"scupper plugs."

Behind the rear seat was a shallow well, doubtless designed to hold a small ice chest but not much more. There was a handle at the stern, another on the bow, and a handle on each side precisely "amidships." (I have always wanted to use that word in print, and now I have. Dreams really do come true.)

Because it was a pedal kayak, it was steered with a hard plastic rudder under the stern. This was turned by thin steel cables that connected to a small tiller on the left side of the rear seat. Because most people are right-handed, and because these boats are primarily used for fishing, the assumption is that the angler would be holding a rod in his right hand and therefore need to steer with his left. In a world where right-handed bias had given me hundreds of obstacles to overcome, just occasionally, that same bias would result in a win for me, and this was one such occasion. The seats, mesh over metal frames, were detachable and could be slid forward or backward on metal rails to adjust for leg length.

The two pedal drives were twenty pounds each, steel, and painted black. A pamphlet in each shipping box touted their virtues:

"The most standing out advantage of this Pedal propellor as follow:

—Light weight
—Energy saving
—Fast speed
—Cost-effective"

Gonna go out on a limb here and guess that these were made in China and that a non-native speaker of English prepared the paperwork. But more on this later.

The drives were identical and interchangeable. Each had a "thwart tube" that ran the width of the cockpit and was held in place by plastic clips on the boat. This thwart tube both held the drive in place and created a hinge effect, allowing the whole affair to be lowered and raised at will. The tube connected to an almond-shaped housing (large at the

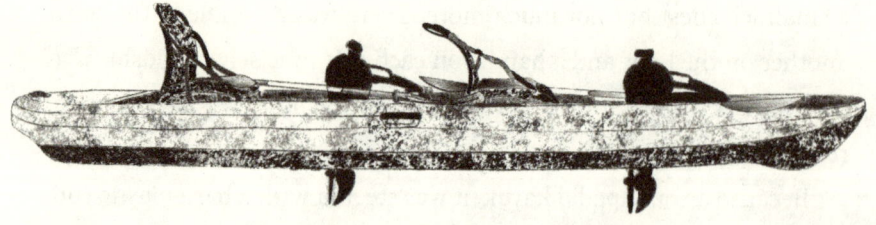

top, small at the bottom). At the top of the housing were the pedals and pedal arms. Hidden inside this housing were the most expensive components of the kayak, the transmission and the gears. Below this housing was a six-inch-deep steel fin—the weed guard. And behind the weed guard, at last, the propeller, one foot in diameter with two blades about two inches wide.

In front of each seat, between one's knees, was the drive well, a hole through to the bottom of the boat, like the scupper holes, but three inches wide and a foot long, allowing one to drop the prop down below the boat and to raise it up again, all from the seated position.

Finally, each drive well had a plastic cover, fastened with elastic shock cords that fit around the drive and prevented water from splashing up through the well into the cockpit.

Everything seemed to fit together just as it should have.

I spent the next week thinking through how to safely get the boat to water. That meant going to the auto parts store and buying ratchet straps to hold the fourteen-foot vessel snug in the bed of my truck, which was eight feet with the tailgate down. For readers who are not up for math, that meant that a full six feet of boat stuck out of the bed, so an old orange dove-hunting vest served nicely as a warning flag to help keep distracted drivers from impaling themselves on my kayak, which, after all, *was* camouflaged.

The bigger challenge of transport was getting the boat the seventy-five yards from the parking lot of Brushy Creek Lake, where I intended to try it out, to the water, because there was no boat ramp accessible by vehicle; the lake allowed no motorized boats.

As I reflect on it, I am probably responsible for captaining the three largest boats ever to sail upon this little lake, and if the lake were not so close, I would have much less experience in finding creative ways to get vessels to the water that are normally just backed down a concrete ramp. There was the 8×16-foot raft we walked from the truck in four sections, each the area of a sheet of plywood, then joined at the water's edge. There was the eleven-foot wooden sailboat, for which I built a custom cart out of PVC and a cut-up pool noodle. And now there was this one, the *Compton Comet*, fourteen feet of gray camo sweetness. For Christmas, my mother-in-law, Phyllis, had sprung for a "universal" kayak cart, and, knowing I was itching to get to the water, she gave it to me a few days early.

After inspecting the 'yak for about a week in our front room, on Christmas Day I asked Andrew to go out on the lake with me. An Eagle Scout, varsity swimmer, and Red Cross-certified lifeguard, he was the best person I knew to help me if something went wrong, and he lived under the very same roof.

After the opening of presents, phone calls to relatives, and lunch, we loaded the *Compton Comet* into the bed of my white Chevy pickup and ratchet-strapped it down. The blaze-orange ratchet-straps worked well—in fact, almost too well: We loaded the boat in backwards so that the slightly tapered bow was the part sticking out. We then hooked the bow handle to the steel loops built into the back corners of my truck's bed, pulled the slack out of the straps, and started cranking. Such was the force of the ratchets that they pulled the kayak, which was already flush with the cab, three inches farther back, stoving in the bed liner at the cab before I even noticed it happening. The *Comet* thus secured, we drove the fifteen minutes to Brushy Creek Lake.

When we reached the lake, it felt odd taking the handicap parking space and yet having the largest, most pimpin' kayak there. As Andrew and I pulled the massive vessel out of the bed and lowered it to the pavement, it looked like a great white shark with extreme rigor mortis. It took up the entire parking lot and blocked every point of egress to the trail that led to the water. What a beautiful sight.

With difficulty, and only by Andrew's force of will, we finally reached the water, unstrapped the boat from its vastly over-burdened cart, lowered ourselves in, and scooched ourselves off the sand.

In the first five minutes on the water, I could do nothing to get my right foot to stay on its pedal. The angle, the exertion required to hold my foot in place, especially with my leg extended, and most of all, the spasticity of my right leg and foot made it impossible. What in the world have I done, I thought. I've just flushed $1,500 down the commode. I guess I'll go home, calmly create a Craigslist account, and start the long and depressing process of clawing back as much of that money as possible. Then I'll have to find some new project in which to immerse myself. Maybe I'll write and illustrate my first anime book. Maybe I'll take up crossbow fishing or one-handed macrame.

Then, Andrew twisted around in the front seat and wrapped the Velcro strap around my shoe. It worked. We took off up the lake at a healthy clip, happily pedaling away.

As we cranked, I wondered aloud about the possibility of just attaching a shoe of some sort directly to the pedal. My Crocs, those famously ugly rubber clogs that looked like they were made of molding Swiss cheese, had a strap across the heel that might be the perfect solution. I had some old Keens sandals that could work too. Andrew said the Croc would be more "meme-able."

When we got back to the takeout, I was first thrilled that I had been able to function in the boat and was confident that I could find some way of keeping my foot on the pedal. At least I now knew that I could get in and out of the boat, and that once my foot got to the pedal, I had the physical wherewithal to make it go.

But that warm, fuzzy feeling was short-lived, because when we tried to get the *Comet* back to the truck, it was incredibly heavy. A look inside the large oval front hatch revealed why. The hull had taken on about five gallons of water, which we poured out when back at the parking lot, along with a lot of thin, curly plastic shavings, the leftovers from the boat's roto-molding manufacturing.

Naturally worried that the boat had a leak, I emailed the company straightaway, and they suggested two methods of determining if there was a crack. One was to wait for nightfall and then shine a light inside the boat to see if any light escaped through cracks or holes. The other was to put the boat up on sawhorses, fill the hull with water and see if any leaked out. Both tests showed no leaks.

Parallel to the quest to keep my foot on the pedal was a quest to figure out how to get the *Comet* from the truck to the water, and how to portage it otherwise. Andrew and I had managed to do it on the virgin voyage, but it was awkward and ugly.

So I spent the week between Christmas and New Year's puzzling over the kayak cart I got from my mother-in-law, which claimed to be "universal" but was definitely not. I had built a PVC cart years earlier to transport my sailing tender, *Hope Floats!,* and so I tried to widen it to fit the kayak's strangely shaped hull. After a long, exhausting morning of gluing, twisting, and pounding the pipes and elbows and T joints into place with only my left hand, I raised the boat up and slowly let it down onto the cart, whereupon the cart flew apart in a heartbreaking clatter of pipes on the driveway. Tears of frustration and rage.

I had not gotten rid of the "universal" cart, and so the following day, I began brainstorming what might make it work. What was needed was not a wider base for the pool noodle runners, but something narrow enough to fit the eight-inch-wide trough that ran down the middle, almost creating the effect of a catamaran. I recalled a long-neglected pool toy in our garage that was something like an underwater skateboard. Called the Sub-Skate, it was the color and texture of a circus peanut. I found it and placed it in the trough. It fit exactly. Needing a tad more height to prevent the wheels from rubbing the bottom of the boat, I shimmed the SubSkate with three short lengths of pool noodle side by side, like a little raft, then lashed it all together with a generous spool of blaze-orange "high visibility" Gorilla Tape.

Trip two to Brushy Creek Lake was with Wade, but it was a bust as I could not keep my foot on the pedal, and the Velcro strap Andrew had used was not working. I might get two or three revolutions, but then *thunk*, my foot would slide off and land in the bottom of the boat like a ringing bass drum. The good news was that at the end of the fifteen-minute trial, the inside of the hull was bone dry. I almost had hoped that it would leak so I could just get the boat replaced and consider the leak issue resolved, but now I could not.

But a floating boat was no good if my right foot would not stay on its pedal.

FIVE

ROLLING IN THE DEEP

"The buoyant force on a body floating in a liquid or gas is also equivalent in magnitude to the weight of the floating object and is opposite in direction..."

—**FROM ARCHIMEDES' PRINCIPLE,
THE LAW OF BUOYANCY**

SIX WEEKS AFTER MY STROKE, I was living in a neuro recovery center, sort of a halfway house for people on the mend from strokes, car and motorcycle accidents, gunshot wounds, and other brain injuries. There, I was clawing my way back into the land of the living with physical therapy.

Often my therapists had me ride a stationary bike, both to rehabilitate my right leg and as a cardiopulmonary workout. I should say they often *tried* to have me ride a stationary bike, but my foot would not stay on the pedal. It was not that my leg was weak; it wasn't. It was that my leg was spastic. Whensoever I really exerted myself, I lost control, and my foot would slip off the pedal as my leg flailed.

Several times, my therapists tried lashing my foot to the pedal with a thin rubbery length of dysum, which is to physical therapy what duct tape is to minor structural failures—the answer to everything, but it never held for more than about ten revolutions of the pedal before my rebellious foot cast off its bonds of oppression and went thudding to the floor.

I'm not sure why I thought the pedal kayak would be any better. Indeed it was worse, because whereas a bicycle pedal is mostly below you, giving your foot at least the advantage of gravity, in a pedal kayak, your foot when fully extended is straight out in front. With the kayak's tiny pedals, experience had shown I had no hope of staying on the pedal more than five revolutions before my foot slid off with a thud against the hollow plastic floor of the cockpit. I knew that if I was to ever get this to work I would need some sort of apparatus supporting the back of my heel, the area just below my Achilles' tendon.

My lifelong friend David is the king of hobbies. Not only have we collaborated on music for more than thirty-five years, every time we got together, it seemed he had just taken up a new hobby. He was a painter. He was a caricaturist. He was a carpenter and aspiring luthier (guitar maker) and was learning calligraphy and welding.

In early February, I was still casting about for a solution to the problem of keeping my right foot on its pedal, and I remembered that a few months earlier, David had taken up leatherworking. So I took one of the pedal drives to his house, explained the problem to him, and left the drive with him to experiment with. Several weeks later he texted me a picture of what he had come up with, and it looked promising: a leather strap that ran behind the heel.

In the first week of March, Dave went with me to the lake to watch as I gave his strap a try. When we reached the water, I took off my ankle brace and set it in the shallow well behind my seat along with the ratchet strap we had used to strap the boat to the cart. There was something a little loose about one of Dave's pedal crank arms, so I unscrewed the hatch below my seat, fished the large allen wrench out of the little red baggie that held the tools, and handed it to Dave. He put a few good cranks on the loose pedal arm and handed the allen wrench back to me. I tossed it back in the baggie, then screwed the hatch lid back on the best I could in my seated position.

As we got underway, it became more or less immediately obvious that the strap, no matter how much we cinched it up, held my foot too low, so that it hit the floor of the cockpit at the bottom of each revolution. I was sad for him. It looked like it would have worked, and it looked cool, too—he had even stamped it with his own leatherworking mark. But it was for naught.

Nevertheless, we had gone to all the trouble of coming out here and did not want to just take the boat straight back to the truck. From the front-seat position, Dave twisted around, and after a mighty struggle on both our parts, he fastened my foot to the pedal with the Velcro strap that came with the drive, just as Andrew had, and we decided to go up the lake and get in a few minutes on the water.

Within about three minutes I noticed the boat listing, to the right. I did not like the look of that, not one bit, so we made a tight turn back toward the boat ramp. Dave started to feel the listing too, and I asked him to lean the opposite way to level us. With the tiller, I angled us toward the bank and began pedaling as fast as I could. But the boat listed more to the left, then more to the left until we were forty-five degrees to the water. This was happening. There was no way around it. About ten feet from the bank, and about fifty yards from the beach, it dumped both of us out, then began sinking in the waist-deep water.

My right foot was still stuck in the Velcro strap on the pedal, and as I was using my left arm to keep my head above water, I could not get it across my body to my right foot. Dave was huffing and puffing as he struggled to stand up in the soft mud and the cold water. He got back to me with a look of utter seriousness on his face, and ripped the strap off my foot.

With our feet finally under us, we dragged the still-sinking boat toward the weedy bank, and Dave managed to climb the bank and hoist the stern onto dry ground. With the boat grounded now, we caught our breath, then began heaving all the flotsam of the wreck ashore—ropes, paddles, my shoes, which I had set behind my chair when I changed into the sandals and now were adrift on the lake.

The hull had now filled with perhaps a hundred pounds of water, and the propeller drives were still locked in the down position. Because the rear of the boat was elevated, I was able to raise the rear drive, unclip it, and hand it ashore to Dave. But the newfound weight of the hull made the front propeller dig into the mud and snapped the submerged blade off like a nacho chip. Dave tugged again on the stern handle and inched the boat higher onto shore, allowing me to rotate the pedals, align the one remaining prop blade with the slot of the drive well, and awkwardly with one hand raise the prop into the boat. Then, with a final desperate heave backward, Dave pulled the *Comet* all the way out of the lake and up a foot to dry, level ground. Deadlifting over one hundred fifty pounds was exactly the wrong call for someone who had undergone surgery for a herniated disc, but he did it, and I was grateful, and embarrassed by the whole tragicomic ordeal I had put him through.

With my feet sinking six inches into soft mud with every step, I stumbled through the water to the bank, then flopped my torso onto the ground like a killer whale beaches itself on that shallow shelf in the Seaworld pool. I lifted my left knee far enough ashore for it to get purchase, then with my left hand grabbed a sturdy clump of weeds and pulled the rest of my body out, got up to kneeling position, got my right knee up, and finally rose to standing.

Now we surveyed the mess. I had not secured anything in the boat and had not even brought the little drybag that hung around my neck. This was a hard lesson learned. Our iPhones, which we both had in our pants pockets, survived, and, incredibly, still worked after being thoroughly submerged. I had set three things behind me in the ice chest well. As mentioned, my shoes floated. The ratchet strap that we used to lash the kayak to the cart was now somewhere at the bottom of the lake. Thankfully, there were three others in the truck.

Most unfortunately, the third thing I had set behind my seat was my ankle-foot orthosis, or AFO—my custom-made ankle brace. And it was gone. This was somewhat inexplicable to me, as it was almost all plastic. "Okay, well that's a real bummer," I said in a low voice, "a *real* bummer." We searched the shoreline for the brace, thinking the wind might have pushed it toward the brushy bank, but nothing. The best I could imagine was that in the scramble, I had stepped on it and forced it so far into the mud that it could not float to the surface. But I thought I would have remembered something like that. A lengthy clean-up and load-out. Apologies. A trip home in wet, muddy clothes. More apologies. Goodbyes. A hot shower. Dejection.

The next morning I awoke early, went to the garage, and found my fishing rod. I located my tackle box, struggled to get it open, and found a large hook and weight, then tied it to the line with my left hand. I returned to the lake with my fishing rod and my three-legged stool, ready to invest an hour or so dragging the hook across the lake bottom in an attempt to salvage the AFO.

When I found the approximate spot where I thought we had gone down, I set my stool down and cast the hook, the first time I had tried casting in more than two years since the stroke, and the first time ever left-handed.

I had not bought a fishing license since the stroke, and as I reeled, I wondered if the fish and game warden who sometimes patrolled this shore would ever believe me when I told him that, despite sitting here and casting a fishing hook into the water over and over again, I was not *actually* fishing. I pictured the conversation, the "fish pig" (as my friends and I had referred to game wardens since high school) standing over me, casually working a toothpick. "So you're not *actually* fishing, huh? What do you call it then?"

"I'm dredging the lake for durable medical equipment. It might *look* like I'm fishing, but it's actually volunteer environmental restoration."

ROLLING IN THE DEEP

By the time I had pulled up the third heaping mass of stringy algae from the bottom, I knew any further effort was a waste of time.

But wait—it felt like plastic and looked like plastic, but was it actually plastic? No, it was resin. Maybe resin didn't float after all. I Googled "Does resin float?" and the answer came in less than half a second: "The general specific gravity of cured epoxy resin is about 1.3. It is heavier than water and will not float."

I had solved the mystery, but that was really neither here nor there. What mattered was that my AFO—my stability—was gone.

Thus the lessons learned from this one twenty-minute outing were three in number: first and foremost, always close the hatches tight—it was because I had opened a hatch to fetch an allen wrench and not properly closed it that the hull had begun taking on water; second, I should never under any circumstances strap any part of myself to the boat; and third, no matter how short the trip, no matter how small or calm the body of water, always use a drybag. Not using a drybag, even on this tiny lake and in shallow water, had been a huge mistake and one I would never repeat.

For a day or two, I considered not replacing the brace. Maybe this was God's way of telling me it was time to finally give it up, this crutch that had become my constant companion.

Forty-eight hours later I was on the phone scheduling an appointment with an orthotist to make a replacement. I was hopelessly dependent on it. Walking without it made me slower than a sloth and was physically and mentally exhausting. For all intents and purposes, the AFO had become part of me.

The COVID-19 shutdown had begun two days earlier, but orthotists, being essential workers, reported to work, and I was hurried through the waiting room and waved to the back.

I made three trips to the orthotist over the coming days—the first for them to cast a fiberglass mold of my leg and foot, the next for me to collect the AFO, and the third for me to get it adjusted after a painful few initial days of walking in it.

On the last trip, I made the acquaintance of the owner of the practice. As I was trying out the brace after his adjustments, we began talking, and I told him that I had been anxiously eager to replace my lost AFO because our Boy Scout troop had planned a campout for the coming weekend that included a five-mile hike, and I knew I couldn't make that distance without the brace. I then described for him my on-again off-again history of using my AFO, and that early on in my stroke recovery, and again after I lost my brace to the lake, I had tried to wean myself off the crutch, but I could not. Going without it was too draining; I was like two different people with and without it.

Then he said something I would not soon forget: Walking without the AFO was not a goal. Hiking five miles with the Boy Scouts—*that* was a goal. It was true, I thought. At the end of the day, I had a choice: walking without a brace but having no energy to do anything else, or walking with the brace and having a life richer in experience.

For the record, not bothering to use a dry bag or lashing my AFO to the boat was a four-hundred-dollar mistake, and also one I would not make again.

SIX

THE SHADE TREE MECHANIC

"Life is 'trying things to see if they work.'"

—**RAY BRADBURY**

AFTER DAVE'S AND MY DUMP, I was on the verge of giving up the dream, and I took several weeks off from even thinking about the trip and the boat and whether I could ever make it all work. But if there's one thing I cannot tolerate, it is the thought of having squandered money. There was the whole irrepressible dream thing too. It was like the old saying "in for a dime, in for a dollar," except the dollar had come first, and it always felt that I was just a dime away from success.

I decided that I would only ever solve the problem of keeping my foot on the pedal if I had a place to work on the modification and try it out at my leisure. The problem had been that for me to be seated in the kayak with the propeller drive down, the boat had to be in the water, and I couldn't take all my tools and experimental materials to the water multiple times and turn the Brushy Creek Lake Park boat ramp into my own personal shipyard.

I needed to have it up off the ground, as I had arranged it in the first days of ownership when I set it up on sawhorses in our front room. But the sawhorses made it too high to get into. Finally a possible solution to the dilemma dawned on me. I happened to have two steel camping cots in the garage. I fetched them down off the top of my plywood storage shelves and set them about eight feet apart in the front yard. (Because of the weirdly shaped lot our house sits on, I could not maneuver the boat into the backyard.) By setting the boat across the cots, I was able to elevate it about a foot off the ground. It was perfect—just low enough for me to climb into and out of, and just high enough so that the prop, when dropped under the boat, still cleared the ground.

This front yard, shade-tree mechanic setup proved to be the turning point in my whole project. There, in the shade of our live oaks, and with all the time in the world now that the pandemic had shut everything else down, I would tinker with this thing until I figured it out.

And it didn't take long. Within about three days I was on my way to a solution. What I needed was some sort of box I could fasten to the pedal. I could see in my mind that was the simplest and perhaps only solution. It was just a matter of finding one or building one and then figuring out how to attach it to the pedal.

It had to be big enough to fit around my sport sandal but not so big that it would allow my foot to turn, and not so wide that it would not clear the wall of the cockpit on its orbit.

After a little online sleuthing, I masked up and went to the home improvement store and thence to the home organization aisle. There, I spotted something that looked about right. It was a bamboo drawer organizer, twelve inches long, six inches wide, and two inches deep. Just to make sure, I set it on the floor and stepped into it like a hardware store Cinderella. It fit just right.

When I got it home, Cameron held it in place on the pedal while I scribed four spots for drill holes. The pedal was steel and had about ten slots running down it. I would feed four bolts through the holes I'd drilled in the tray, and they would continue down through the slots in the pedal, with hand-tightening wing nuts below the pedal holding the whole affair together.

THE SHADE TREE MECHANIC

I tried it out, and it worked. I even shot a video and posted it to Facebook for the few friends who were aware of my quest.

Quickly I texted Wade and scheduled another trip to the lake for the coming Saturday. He met me there, and we got the boat to the water and floated it before sitting in it. Details like getting the boat on and off the circus-peanut cart and floating the boat before sitting in it were things we gradually were working out, in parallel to solving the larger problem of me pedaling the boat.

Maybe it was three revolutions of the pedal or perhaps five, but it wasn't more than ten seconds before the walls of the bamboo-and-plastic drawer organizer split apart and my foot slid off the pedal with a *thunk* on the bottom of the boat.

I let out a profane oath, and despaired. Why had it worked for thirty continuous minutes in my yard but fallen apart immediately on the water? I calmed myself, and we turned to make the forty-foot return to the beach.

It was early in the day, and I had an idea. The concept and the design had worked; this was merely a materials problem. The water that had dripped off my sandal had immediately dissolved the thin bead of glue that held the bamboo edges to the plastic floor of the box. If I could get that shape in a new material, problem solved.

Wade and I moved the kayak back to the parking lot and set it next to my truck. An Asian American man who was walking past saw the boat, raised his phone, squatted down, and snapped a photo. It took small moments like this to remind me that the boat really was something to behold, as I had accrued almost nothing but feelings of frustration toward it from the first time I had put it on the water.

Trusting that no one would have the audacity to steal it with the ambiguity of my truck right next to it, Wade and I climbed into his car and made our way four miles back to the home improvement store. There, I strode to the home organization aisle and again to the drawer organizer section. Six feet over from the same bamboo box that now lay in pieces in Wade's car, I spotted a box of the exact same dimensions molded out of thick, clear plexiglass. I grabbed it and headed to checkout, almost without breaking stride. The box looked very much like a casserole dish, and that is what it was known as from then on.

From there, we drove to my house, where we used the bottom of the busted bamboo box as a template to drill matching holes in the casserole dish. Then we returned to the lake. A gust of wind had turned the boat over on its cart, but after righting it and gathering the paddles and straps that had spilled out, we successfully attached the casserole dish to the pedal with the four bolts and wing nuts, took it back to the water, and we were off.

We made it the quarter mile up the lake and the quarter mile back. It was a success. At last, I thought, we're on our way.

SEVEN

THE SHAKEDOWN

A little learning is a dangerous thing;
Drink deep, or taste not the Pierian spring:
There shallow draughts intoxicate the brain,
And drinking largely sobers us again . . .

—ALEXANDER POPE,
"A LITTLE LEARNING"

I HAD ALWAYS HELD that the next critical step on the journey would be the shakedown, a sort of dress rehearsal for the main event.

It was a remnant of my experience as a Boy Scouts dad. In scouting, there are two types of campouts—regular and high adventure. A typical Boy Scout might go on ten regular campouts a year. These are normally two nights: leave on Friday afternoon and get back Sunday at one. High adventure trips, on the other hand, happen once or twice a year, mostly in the summer. These are often in some faraway place and last for two weeks at a time.

There are three primary high adventure camps in the United States: Sea Base, a sailing camp in the Florida Keys; Northern Tier, a canoeing trip in the boundary waters between Minnesota and Canada; and the largest of all, Philmont, a hiking trip in the Rocky Mountains of New Mexico. As an adult leader, I had only been able to go on one such high adventure trip before having my stroke, and that one was Philmont, with Andrew.

On the lead-up to Philmont, the Scouts and adults who were going met numerous times for brutal hikes up and down stairs on a greenbelt in the hills of west Austin. We hiked with our loaded packs on to simulate and acclimate to the hard work Philmont would be. We even went on a whole regular campout in preparation for Philmont to dial in our equipment and be sure we had what we needed.

The shakedown was thus deeply embedded in my thinking about outdoor adventure, and I knew that we needed a shakedown now even more than I did for Philmont. There was a lot to test. So I talked Wade into a one-night trip, a proof-of-concept that would no doubt tell us many things, primarily what we really needed to take on the Nueces trip and what we shouldn't bother with.

We chose a familiar stretch of the Colorado River just below Austin, the same fifteen-mile section we had done on the Sterilite bin raft with our boys five years earlier. We knew the highway bridge where we would put in. We knew the large island where we could camp overnight. And we knew the city park in Bastrop where we would take out. We had our hands full with other unknowns—like my seaworthiness and physical ability to handle the river and Wade's relative inexperience with boating. Having these givens gave us just enough to forge ahead and learn the next set of lessons we would need to make the big trip.

With Kirstin along to drive the truck home, we pulled up at eight o'clock, and with her help, rolled the boat down the ramp and carried down all the gear. Local black and brown folks were fishing for catfish under the bridge with shrimp, a bait choice we had never heard of for freshwater and which reinforced my theory that everything in nature loves to eat shrimp, whether they know it from their natural habitat or not. You could approach a bison with a handful of shrimp, and the landlocked herbivore would happily eat it, and perhaps ask if there was any cocktail sauce.

We successfully launched the *Compton Comet* fitted with the casserole dish, with the drybag, circus-peanut cart, and five-gallon bottomless potty bucket in tow.

It was my first time in the kayak on a river, and it was a beautiful mid-May morning—egrets crossing the river, turtles plopping off logs as we approached. "This is the finest thing in life," I proclaimed, ". . . besides love and kids and all that."

"I don't know," Wade said, "there are days when it's even better than those."

"Whatever it is, it beats sitting at the desk," I said.

"Amen."

One crucial piece of equipment I had yet to try was the LifeStraw. The plan was not to carry clean water with us on the trip, as that would have added an inordinate amount of weight. Rather, we would reach overboard, scoop nasty water right out of the river, and drink it through LifeStraws.

LifeStraws had been on the market about ten years by then, and the commercials showed rugged hikers on their bellies drinking out of crystal-clear streams through their straws. LifeStraws came in different forms, and mine attached to the screw-on lid of my one-liter Nalgene bottle. I screwed the lid off with one hand and, gripping the bottle tightly, dragged it along the water's surface for about two seconds.

Raising it up toward the sun, the light of that main-sequence star barely made it through. The liquid looked more like the chai tea lattes Kirstin loved, or like chocolate Nehi, than like the streams on the LifeStraw ads. I lowered the lid-mounted straw into the fluid (I won't call it water) and screwed the lid tight. Then, with a deep breath and visions of parasites, viruses, bacteria, and explosive diarrhea dancing in my head, I raised the straw to my lips and sucked. Not bad. A little weird, but more in the way that distilled water tastes weird than like algae tastes weird. Success. The LifeStraw concept worked, and we would be spared the burden of toting potable water.

Right about then, we looked down the river and saw two things: a high bluff dead ahead that signaled a hairpin turn in the wide river, and a dramatic change in the river's surface, almost a boiling. We watched the approaching turbulence with interest and tried to find our best line through the sharp turn. I had just made a hard right with the rudder when we felt the boat hit the rocky bottom and heard a tremendous scraping. We lodged on a grassy island in the river as we both struggled to get our propellors up through their slotted wells, trying multiple times to move the pedals so as to align the two prop blades at twelve and six o'clock to thread the props up through the wells.

My prop came up first into the boat. No damage. When we finally got Wade's prop up, one of the two blades had snapped clean off, just as it had when the boat sank with Dave and me in March. We were less than thirty minutes into the trip.

When we reached depth, we pressed on. Wade was able to get some decent thrust out of his sad single-blade propeller, which of course now created strange vibrations below the boat, as if the *Compton Comet* had a broken motor mount.

When we had made the rafting trip five years earlier, we had reached the island to make camp about five in the afternoon. This day, with a healthy current from an overnight rain and a boat that could actually be steered, we reached the same island, where we had planned to stay the night, at noon.

Well, I thought, we'll have a leisurely afternoon to really dial in our camping form. The sun was high, and so I thought the first thing to do would be to set up the tarp I had brought. I pictured us having long hours in the sun on our big trip and needing shade but not wanting to sit inside the tent. So I had brought a tarp and my two collapsible aluminum poles so that we could stake the tarp up at an angle and sit on the lightweight hiking chair and the stool in its shade.

THE SHAKEDOWN

We laid out the tarp, laid out the poles, and I talked Wade through where I thought we should place the stakes. Sitting on my three-legged stool with him crouching over, I had been teaching him the tautline hitch for about ten minutes when he suddenly said, "Dude, look at the back of the boat."

Wade had pulled the boat completely onto dry land thirty minutes earlier, but now the stern was sitting in four inches of water. We both stood up and started leisurely toward the boat, and when we were about fifteen feet away, the rear swung smoothly out into the swiftly moving river. Wade grabbed it by the stern handle and muscled it back up onto still higher ground on the island.

A wave of adrenaline washed over me. It was one of those moments when the relief of a rescue comes first, and the full realization of what was rescued comes after. I had no time to rejoice in Wade's saving the boat because of the sickening realization that we had come just five seconds from 1. losing the boat completely, 2. losing the big trip for which we were preparing, and 3. being stranded, 3a. on an island amid a rapidly rising river, and 3b. in an area we couldn't have described how to get to if we had needed to be picked up, after a journey of unknown length to even find a road. Five seconds from being profoundly screwed in four or five different ways.

Dave had rescued the boat after it sank. Wade had rescued it from being washed away. If the disastrous outing with Dave was inoculation one, this was inoculation two: we would never again assume the river level was static, especially if it had rained upstream within the last twenty-four hours, and we would never again assume the boat was safe unless it was tied fast to something really solid.

Wade placed a stick at the water's edge, and we ate lunch while we watched the stick slowly be devoured by the rising river. We had wanted to camp there overnight, to work out any bugs in our gear, determine if we hadn't brought anything that we actually needed, or, almost of equal importance in light of our limited storage, if we had brought something we didn't need. But the water was still rising, and almost losing the boat had quickly recalibrated my thinking. I still had one bar of reception on my cell phone, so I used it to pull up the website of the Lower Colorado River Authority. It just so happened that the island where we were was one hundred feet away from a river depth gauge that we could see nestled in the trees on the bank, and the data was being updated every ten minutes on the website. That data was confirming what the stick was telling us: the river was still rising.

Our proximate goal was camping that night, but the ultimate goal was the big trip, and I did not want to risk the big goal for the little one. The broken prop, the close call with the boat, and the uncertainty of river conditions upstream and weather conditions in the Colorado River's watershed—perhaps we had learned enough for one day. I determined the smarter play was to live to pedal another day.

We loaded up the gear as huge logs and downed snags swiftly floated past us in the chocolate-milk water, got our life jackets on, and shoved off again.

One thing we had brought along that we decided we did not need was the tarp and the poles that supported it. We would be too tired to set that up, and besides, we would not be making camp at noon; we would be making camp at six or seven in the evening and would have little need for a tarp then.

We reached Bastrop at three-thirty that afternoon, and poor Kirstin would not only *not* have the bed to herself that night but would have to make two roundtrips in one day to East Central Texas.

～～～

The one thing we had learned that we needed and did not have was better back support. Throughout the afternoon, Wade had been wincing and complaining that his lower back was in pain from the recumbent angle at which we sat. This was a relatively short day on the water, so the fact that he was already in pain did not bode well if we were to be on the water all day every day for the better part of the week. This would need to be addressed.

Wade said he might get a back brace similar to the ones grocery stockers use. The next day, he sent me a link with what he intended to buy, and I told him to go ahead and throw one in the cart for me, too. The website showed two guys smiling ear to ear with back braces, knee braces, and elbow braces on. "We could be like Brett and Jerry," Wade texted.

I texted him back, "These guys look pretty happy for being as banged up as they are!" Only later did I realize I was looking at Brett Favre and Jerry Rice. We wouldn't be getting sacked by three-hundred-pound linebackers or laying out for a reception, but if Copper brand braces were good enough for these G.O.A.T.s, we were in.

The timing of the trip had been left up in the air. Maybe this spring, maybe early summer, possibly fall or even next spring, whenever we felt ready and had the chance.

The one variable that drove the decision more than anything was the lack of cargo space on the boat. Cool nights would necessitate bulky sleeping bags, and we simply had no room for those, or coats or anything else cold nights call for.

Wade had a weeklong sales retreat (on Zoom) that started June 11. If we waited until after that, South Texas would be unbearably hot and probably too dry to float a boat.

What's more, most of the gear we would take, even the food we would eat, had already been packed or bought for the shakedown. Waiting six months or a year would mean that we would mentally have to go through every checklist again to make sure we were taking the right provisions.

Moreover, I knew in my gut that if we waited months or another year to make the big trip, parts of the boat itself would start to fall apart. The metal rails that held the seats had already begun to rust in the elements. The plastic hull, exposed to the heat and cold and moisture as it was, would start to fade and maybe even become brittle.

Finally, ironically, the COVID-19 pandemic shutdown had created a perfect window for us to get out and do this, as it had eliminated any competition for our time outside of work. We no longer had to thread the needle of family vacations and taking children to camp or off to college. The coronavirus had reduced our activity to sitting at home working and sitting at home watching TV.

We should go now, I thought. We should go. My preparation now took on an air of urgency.

EIGHT

THE LAYING ON OF EYES

"Seeing is believing, but feeling is the truth."
—THOMAS FULLER

AS I HAVE TRIED TO MAKE CLEAR, I had no death wish, and while I longed to do something audacious and to have a genuine adventure, I had a greater desire to live to tell about it and also to not let the trip descend from adventure into misery. I could handle misery by myself—I was by now an old hand at it. What I could not stomach was the thought of putting Wade through misery if I could prevent it. I knew there would be hardship, but when we looked back on it years later, I wanted us both to remember the trip fondly, not with post-traumatic stress.

Anyone who might be mulling a similar adventure should appreciate the extent to which I prepared. As should already be clear, I did not just up and decide to do a river trip one day to show my stroke who was boss. For more than six months, I spent a large fraction of all my waking hours thinking through this trip, solving problems related to doing it with a serious disability, and safeguarding us as much as humanly possible against calamity.

The first key to planning had to be getting an accurate measurement of how far we would be going.

Since childhood, I had carried a memory that loomed large in my thinking about this trip. When I was eight, my dad bought a canoe kit and took over our dining room for two weeks to assemble it. It was pink vinyl stretched over a light wooden fuselage frame. If IKEA sold canoes, this is what they might look like and how they'd be put together.

When it was done, we strapped it to the top of our station wagon and took it to Delta Lake near Elsa to try it out. On our way home, we were cruising at highway speed when a drunk driver tried to cross the road in front of us. We T-boned him and flipped him onto his roof. The canoe broke free of the rope Dad had tied it down with and sailed off the station wagon fifty feet or more down the highway. The Mercury station wagon, pea-soup green with faux wood paneling (yes, just like the one in *Vacation*), was totaled, and promptly replaced by a powder-blue Plymouth Gran Fury station wagon. As for the canoe, it was banged up but fared better than the car, and with a few new screws and some red vinyl patches over the pink vinyl skin, it was ready for whatever water we could find in this arid country.

My memories of paddling the pink canoe gravitate to a particularly rainy September. It rained unceasingly for probably a week, and the motocross park a block from our house filled up like a lake. Dave and I carried the pink canoe over there along with a small trident I had bought for gigging frogs. We had fun paddling in the "lake," but if memory serves, no frogs were harmed in the making of that particular adventure.

Dad then tapped my oldest brother, Ansen, then in junior high school, to go with him on a day-trip down the Rio Grande.

Things started to go off the rails when late in the morning Dad came down with a splitting headache and had to lie back in the boat and leave all the paddling to Ansen. But the real problem was that Dad had grossly underestimated the distance. Surely he knew it would be farther on the river than as the crow flies, but he clearly did not understand how exponentially farther river miles can be than highway miles, as the river mercilessly meanders and doubles back on itself, heading east only slightly more than every other direction, as if actively trying to avoid the Gulf.

THE LAYING ON OF EYES

It was near dark when he and Ansen reached the ferry at Los Ebanos and could take out. Ansen grabbed hold of the steel cable that spanned the river, which was used to pull the hand-drawn ferry back and forth, and narrowly avoided capsizing. Dad talked a good-hearted local into driving them into town and found a convenience store pay phone to call my mother, who was by that time apoplectic with worry that they were both dead. It had taken them all day to go precisely half the distance planned.

That memory, and our near loss of the boat on our shakedown trip, had caused me to think more seriously about extraction.

I don't know what research if any Dad did before his and Ansen's Rio Grande day trip turned into a day-and-night trip, but I know one thing: I now had a powerful planning tool Dad never could have dreamed of—Google Maps.

Google Maps had been around since 2003, when CNN started using its predecessor, Keyhole, to zoom in on bombing targets during the Iraq War. The map layers allowed one to toggle between highway maps and satellite photos and to zoom in with remarkable resolution that showed not only highways and marked roads but dirt paths, islands in the river and oxbow lakes, gravel bars and low dams and rocky outcroppings and little foot bridges that would never show up on a merely geographic map.

Most importantly, Google Maps allowed you to make point-to-point measurements simply by clicking a measuring stick and then clicking on the river, clicking to set a new point every time the river curved. And so I spent a total of probably fifteen hours over many weeks repeatedly measuring the river. Not understanding the tool entirely, I once spent nearly an hour scrolling my way down the river setting points and tracing the river all the way to the Gulf, only to click off of the tool and lose the entire thing. They say measure twice and cut once, but this was ridiculous. Not wanting to lose my meticulous measurements again, the next time I broke the river into five-mile segments, and each time I measured another five miles, I would drop a pin and label it—"Mile 30" or "Mile 65" or what have you.

This was key, because now I at least had a rough idea of how far it was and then could estimate how long it could take, though this estimate remained fluid for the duration of the trip. Nevertheless, I now had a range. If we could only make ten miles a day, it would take more than eight days. If we made twenty-five miles a day, we'd be done in fewer than four. A wide range, but at least we had a range now, and not just a shrug.

~~~

Four years earlier, I had hiked the Lone Star Trail, a hundred-mile path through the Sam Houston National Forest in East Texas. For that, the internet readily served up a set of detailed notes describing landmarks along the way and cautions to turn this way or that. These notes, in addition to the highly visible mile markers and the trail blazes, left little doubt where I was and how much progress I had made.

There was not much chance of getting lost on the river; it had that over the forest in spades. But there were no mile markers. And I could find no such notes for the Nueces River comparable to trail notes. So I decided to create my own.

I scrolled down the river looking for any landmark we could see from the water. If I could see that a creek entered the river, I would measure forward or backward from the nearest five-mile pin and add it to my list in order: "Mile 12: large Para Creek enters river-left" ". . . Mile 55, houses start on right" ". . . Mile 72, railroad bridge." This would allow us to know roughly where we were on the river, even without GPS. Phones die. Phones can be dropped in the river.

The last benefit to come from our shakedown trip on the Colorado was extraction directions. Indeed, how would someone know where to extract us if we lost the boat, if the drives jammed or we broke all the propellers we had, or one of us got bitten by a snake or an alligator? What if Wade had chest pains or if I had a seizure? (I had taken daily seizure medicine since my stroke and the seizure that sent me into emergency brain surgery.)

So I identified every spot along the way from which we could be picked up if the need arose. Most were bridges, but some were points where a road came unusually close to the river. Once I had found a potential extraction point, I mapped the closest route from I-37 to that point, which was usually less than ten miles and fewer than four turns away. If we had to tap out, I could tell Kirstin which extraction point we were closest to, and she would have the best route from home all ready to go, from the highway exit number to the river. Some part of me felt that the extent of this meticulous preparation virtually assured that we would not need it—some sort of reversal or corollary of Murphy's Law.

I was perhaps most nervous about the river not being deep enough for the boat. Fully loaded, we drafted about twenty inches; the boat itself rode about eight inches into the water, and the propeller protruded beneath the boat exactly a foot. I just didn't know, and could never know absolutely, if the river was navigable all the way down; boating the length of this river was just not something that was done on any sort of a regular basis. There was no Facebook group for Nueces paddlers, no club of enthusiasts we could plug into. Even data on the Lower Nueces River Authority website did not tell us anything of much use. At length, I decided the only way I was going to achieve at least a level of comfort that would allow me to go was to lay eyes on the river at as many points as possible and, because river levels can change dramatically over time, to lay eyes on it within a week of the trip.

Wade agreed to go with me. We left early on a Saturday morning and drove to our planned put-in at George West. The river there certainly appeared deep enough. The first bridge, at mile six, appeared to be built of railroad ties and offered no real access to the river if there had been an emergency. I scratched it off my list of extraction points. A section a little farther down appeared wide, slow and shallow, with numerous snags protruding above the water. We noted the blue heron wading only knee-deep fifty yards out into the lazy river. This concerned me greatly, but I convinced myself there was a river channel somewhere out there that would give us our twenty inches of draft.

At the south end of Lake Corpus Christi, we spent more than an hour investigating potential portages around the dam that created the lake, driving backroads, looking at satellite images on our phones, walking foot trails created by local fishermen. The dam itself and all the property around it was fenced off. A padlocked gate sported a sign with two phone numbers we could call. We copied them down, and Wade scouted a quarter-mile path to a steep sidewalk that led down to the river.

Farther downstream, we crossed the river on the Highway 666 Bridge, the Bridge of the Beast. A little farther down, now within Corpus Christi city limits, we drove through a county park, and annotated the river notes with the handwritten exclamation, "Trash Cans!" Ten minutes later we were making a U-turn under I-37 to scope the second and final portage at Calallen Dam, a small spillway made of concrete and rubble that looked very manageable. Our attempt to spot the river's mouth from the road was obscured by industrial levees.

I felt good about the scouting trip, and it gave us both peace of mind about some stretches and concerns about others. There was less than one week left.

NINE

SLOW BOAT FROM CHINA

*"The superior man understands what is right;
the inferior man understands what will sell."*

—CONFUCIUS

WHEN I GOT HOME from the scouting trip, I edited my river notes, deleting the places where extraction was not possible. Once the list had been tightened up to its essentials, I shrank it to six-point type, printed it out, cut it up, and mounted it on two index cards, front and back. Kirstin found some see-through contact paper that effectively laminated the cards, and they went in a pocket of my life jacket for easy reference.

That week, I worked the phones, first calling the city of Corpus Christi about the dam. When I finally got through to the dam manager (I have always wanted to say that), he told me there was no way to come near enough to the dam to portage around it with the circus peanut because we could not come inside the buoys. I hadn't even noticed this buoy line on satellite before, but on reinspection, there it was, a line of white dots all the way across the lake.

He did offer that we could take out at an RV park that the city also operated at the north end of the dam called Sunrise Beach, but we would need a vehicle to make that portage, as it would be some four miles out of the park, around the dam, and back down to the river.

Kirstin was already making two roundtrips to South Texas in less than a week, one to drop us off and one to pick us up, for a total of twelve hours on the road. She would have made a third had I asked her, but I couldn't in good conscience. So I called one of my two older brothers, Erren, who lived in our hometown of McAllen, to see if he would rendezvous with us at Lake Corpus Christi and, with his truck, help us portage from Sunrise Beach to some spot below the dam. He agreed.

With that major detail resolved, the primary stressor became finding spare props. We had snapped one blade of a propeller during the shakedown, and I had not been able to find a replacement. We absolutely could not make this trip without at least one full spare prop and preferably two or three. And now that our vacation leave time had been approved, and we could not delay, finding a prop became a race against the clock.

Austin's kayak store said they would have them in three days, but when I looked at their website the following day, the arrival date for the back-ordered props had already shifted to the day before we were leaving. I had to do better.

I was willing to pay overnight shipping from anywhere in North America for the props. A website for a store in Delaware showed them in stock, but I was not confident they could really arrive in time. Nor did I have much confidence anymore that these website inventories were accurate.

Everything was back-ordered nationwide. The coronavirus pandemic had supply chains across the globe completely jacked up, especially things coming from the country where everything was made, including the virus—China. How strange that of all things, what was bringing the global pandemic home for me was not that grocery stores were out of flour. It was not that I had gotten sick, or even knew anyone who had; it was that I could not find a replacement propeller for my pedal kayak. *Now* shit was getting real!

After my first prop break, when the boat sank under Dave and me, I had ordered a replacement from a store in Dallas, so I called it back.

They had to check the warehouse and call me back, but yes, they had two. They were a little shorter, but shorter props would fit. I would take them both. They shipped them that day, and I received them the next.

The pandemic had another effect aside from a massive supply-chain breakdown, of course. It stripped small businesses to the bone, and almost overnight, business owners were answering their own phones and filling orders themselves, just trying to make the next month's rent. So it was that I had gotten an especially knowledgeable kayak store owner on the phone in Dallas, and I picked his brain.

"The drive I've got is not Native Watercraft," I said, "in fact it doesn't even have a brand name on it, but I notice that only Native Watercraft makes the replacement parts. I guess what I got was a Chinese imitation of some sort, huh?"

"Well," he said, "it's not really an imitation, it's theft."

Of course. It wasn't that some collection of industrious Chinese citizens had been inspired by the Native Watercraft design and decided to create something similar. They had bought a Native Watercraft drive, taken it apart, scanned every component—or perhaps just stolen the specs off a server—and replicated every last gear, housing, fitting, joint, weld, nut, and bolt down to a micrometer.

It was clear as day now. The hilariously poor English in the assembly instructions: "The most standing out features are . . . " The cheap pot metal cracking. The great price that had drawn me to the Outer Banks website to begin with, which in turn kept serving up ads for the 14TPK until I relented—it was all part of a bigger story, one I should have guessed. Chinese intellectual property theft was not something that only happened to movie and music distributors, getting undersold by knock-offs in seedy bazaars. It was everywhere, costing the United States by some estimates $600 billion a year, and I now owned a prime example of it. I felt dirty for having enabled this theft, but I hadn't known, and anyway, there was nothing to do about it now.

THE RIVER NUTS

On the Monday before we were to leave, I was in the garage inspecting the drives for some reason and did a slow double-take of something that looked wrong. In front of each propeller was supposed to be a heavy steel fin, the weedguard. And on one of the drives, it was simply gone, cracked off in a jagged break that would give the prop blades no protection from a rocky bottom, never mind sweeping weeds out of the way so they would not be wound up in the prop. It must have been cracked when we grounded out on the shakedown, and then broken off in the truck bed as we rode home, with no one noticing it was gone as we put it up on its plywood shelf.

Well, shit. I had to move heaven and earth to find spare props, the replacement part that should be the most plentiful, and now that I found spare propellers, the thing that protects the propellers from immediately snapping off is gone. Is the universe trying to tell me something? Is the universe trying to keep me from making this trip? Or is the universe merely testing my will, seeing how badly I really want it?

The replacement weedguard, assuming I could even find it at the eleventh hour, was one hundred dollars. But by now I was a seasoned veteran of hardware store modifications, and not having access to a welding rig, this was all I could think to do: There was just enough steel—if we can call it that—to drill a hole and bolt something to it that would serve the same purpose. Back to Lowe's I went, returning home with a drill bit made for steel, two bolts, two nuts, and a thin steel L bracket used for joining boards at a right angle.

In the garage, I clamped the L into my workbench vice and somehow switched out the blade on my sawzall for the hacksaw blade. With one hand trying to control the wildly vibrating reciprocating saw, I managed to make three cuts to get the brace down to usable size. Then, having had enough solo fun for one day, I held the unwieldy drive upside down while Cameron, my sixteen-year-old, drilled the holes, inserted the bolts, and tightened down the nuts. It sure wasn't pretty, but it held. The last fix was in place. The boat would go.

But there was one last mod I felt the vessel needed. I had ordered the boat in gray camouflage because I thought it looked cool, but nearly from the moment my cursor left the "Purchase" button, I had regretted the choice, especially when I considered being on a lake at sunrise with an unknown number of motor boats. So I asked Ian, my thirteen-year-old, to come out to the front yard and help me. I handed him a giant roll of high-visibility orange duct tape, and we proceeded to wrap the boat all the way around its perimeter with a single length of tape. This final mod was a little bit like putting a ribbon around a gift. There was nothing left to do.

The next day, another high school friend, Ed, dropped by the house with a graduation present for Andrew and some University of Houston branded swag for Kirstin and me. His family stayed in the car, and he kept his mask on as we visited briefly in the front yard. His questions mirrored the questions I still had: he had looked at Google satellite images too. "There are sections that look pretty shallow. Are you sure you can make it down the river?"

"Nope," I said, "not really sure of anything, but I think we'll survive."

It was the first time he had seen the boat in person, and as an avid fisherman and the owner of several kayaks himself, he was impressed by the *Compton Comet*. "You're not worried about someone stealing it out here?"

"Nah," I said. "We're pretty safe here on our little cul-de-sac, no through-traffic."

"You might want to run a bike lock through one of those scupper holes and chain it to the tree."

"That's a good idea." I said, before he said goodbye, wished us luck, and drove away. The boat had been sitting out here in the front yard, propped up on my two cots, for more than two weeks while I worked on it. I was sure it would be fine for the remaining couple of days.

That night, Kirstin had trouble sleeping and so went to our front dining room to read. It was about two-thirty in the morning when she saw the headlights of a car idling in the cul-de-sac. When she peeked through the blinds, she saw an unfamiliar station wagon, just sitting there. She quickly turned on the porch light, and the car drove away. The next morning, with only a few days left, I lifted the drives out and put them in the garage, strapped the boat to the circus peanut cart, and moved the whole affair back inside the gate and into the boatport.

I had cheated fate one more time.

TEN

THE FINAL COUNTDOWN

"A ship is safe in harbor, but that's not what ships are for."
—WILLIAM G. T. SHEDD

IN THE TIME BETWEEN the shakedown trip and the big trip, I could feel anxiety rising in my chest, and my emotions vacillated between excitement and a very real fear of the abyss, a fear of not coming back. It was an echo of the anxiety I felt at the run-up to my solo hike across Sam Houston National Forest.

It is an odd mental space to be in—to feel dread over something that is completely voluntary. No one but me cared in the least whether I went through with this or not. If I had thought better of the whole thing, Wade might have been disappointed for five or ten minutes, but then he would have gone on with his busy life without giving it another thought. He was all in, but I knew in the final analysis he basically was doing this as a favor to an old friend and that he himself had no lifelong urge to camp down a river to the sea.

I live my life as a book with chapters. And the chapters have to be finished for the book to go on. And there has to be rising action, and there has to be struggle in the pursuit of a goal. If I had spent all this money and time in pursuit of this goal and somehow couldn't make it work, or got too freaked out by the prospect of getting hurt or dying, then this chapter of my life would be a dud, a rabbit hole that went nowhere, an eddy. I just had to take the leap, no matter if I couldn't see the other side. That's what protagonists do.

But suddenly, something happened that crowded that anxiety out.

Andrew had graduated from high school the previous week. It should have been a momentous rite of passage, but the coronavirus pandemic had converted it into a footnote. His big day was marked by the five of us filing into the district's high school football stadium, walking down the sideline to the far end zone, and him walking across a stage and pausing for a photo as an announcer read his name to an empty stadium and whoever might have been watching the livestream.

Now he was just two weeks away from beginning online summer school, and he decided it was his birthright as an American to take a road trip after graduating high school. We put only two stipulations on the trip. The first was that he not go alone, so he hastily texted a friend who agreed to make the trip with him. They would leave in forty-eight hours. The second stipulation was that he download the Find My iPhone app so that we could see where he was.

He laid out an audacious itinerary. Day one was Austin to Roswell, New Mexico. Day two, the Grand Canyon. Days three and four, San Diego. Day five, Lake Tahoe. Days six and seven, Idaho to visit the other boy's family. Day seven, Glacier National Park in Montana. Day eight, Mount Rushmore. From there, it would be on to Minneapolis, for some reason I could never quite discern; then they'd play it by ear—perhaps the Smoky Mountains, back through the swamps of Louisiana, and home to Austin before classes started.

Did I mention that Andrew had never before driven for more than an hour at a stretch? I wondered where in the world he got the audacity to try a crazy trip like that.

Be all that as it was, Kirstin and I were both rooting for him, desperately wanting it to work out, wanting him to have an authentic adventure, wanting him to get out of the house where he had been stuck in lockdown since March 13. But surely you can feel the storm of mixed emotions we both had, watching one of our three most beloved things in the world, green and tender in our eyes, drive off on a trip that would have been very challenging even in normal times, but now was off into a scary America the rules of which seemed to be changing by the minute.

Suddenly, with less than a week to go to my trip, most of my worrying had been siphoned away by his trip. At dawn the day before we were to leave for South Texas and the Nueces, Kirstin and I sat on the porch and waved goodbye to Andrew as he drove away in Kirstin's white Subaru in the direction of Roswell. Seated in our matching white rocking chairs, we held hands and smiled with tightly closed lips as tears streamed down our cheeks. What terrifying joy, this parenting thing.

I had decided to leave for the trip Friday night so that we could be on the water early and therefore get a full day's pedaling in on day one. Wade, Kirstin, and I left around six and made our way through Austin, San Marcos, New Braunfels, San Antonio, and thence into The Nothing.

We arrived in George West, population 2,480, about nine, and just catty-corner to the Dairy Queen we had patronized perhaps more than a hundred times, we found the Best Western hotel at which I had reserved a room.

As I checked in, the TV above the front desk, tuned to Fox News, proclaimed in the lower-third Chyron "PROTESTS AND LOOTING ACROSS AMERICA." A split screen showed live looting in Atlanta and protests in Minneapolis over the death of George Floyd earlier that week. I was glad to be getting on the water and away from my newsfeed, and my mind turned to Andrew, who was somewhere in the Southwest that night, sleeping in our car in a hotel parking lot so that he could get a glimpse of the Grand Canyon the next day.

PART II

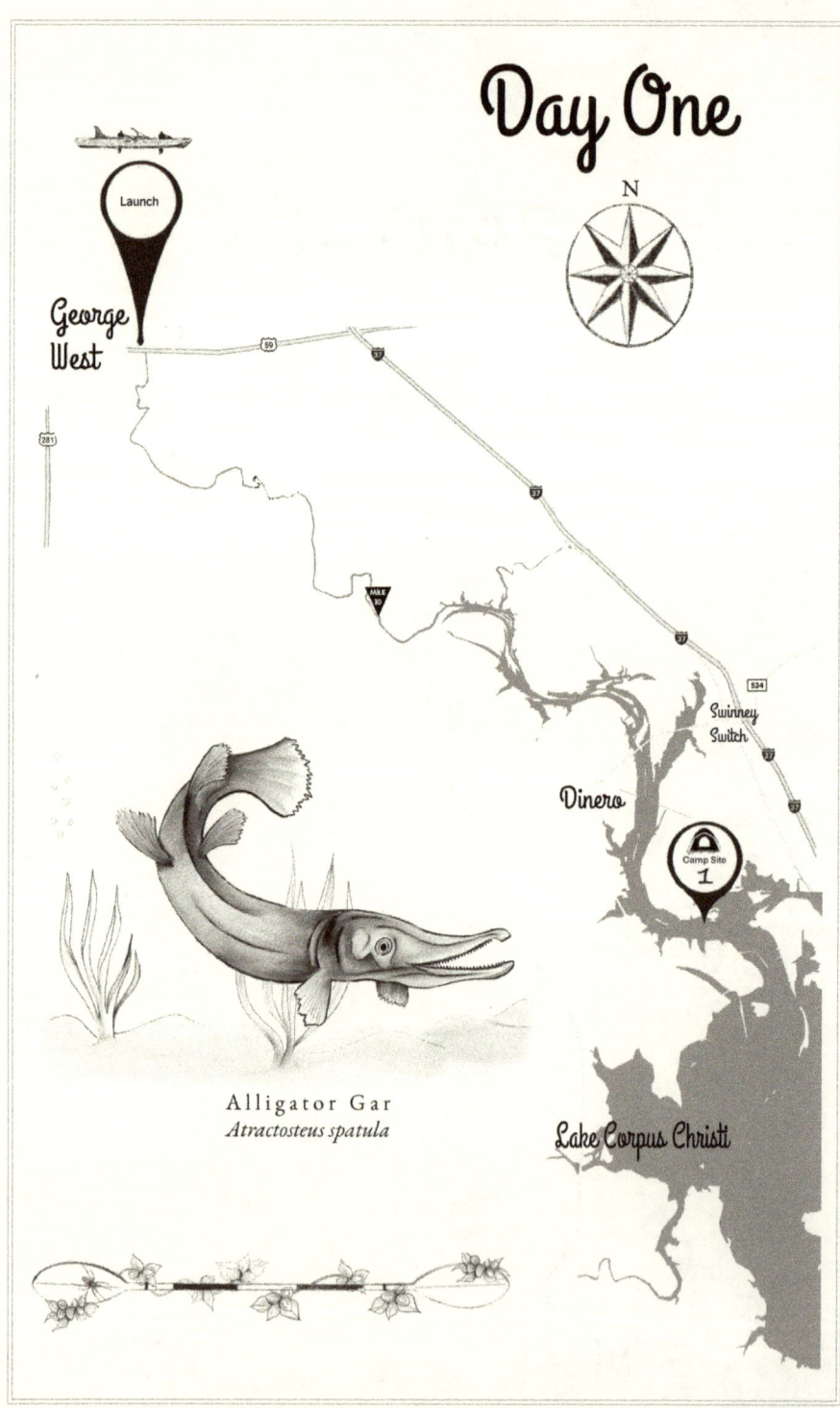

ELEVEN

ÁNDA!

"I leave this rule for others when I'm dead
Be always sure you're right — THEN GO AHEAD!"
—DAVY CROCKETT

NEARLY EVERY BATHROOM SINK has an overflow drain, a slot-like hole near the top of the sink's front edge. Since my stroke, I had become a huge fan of these holes, not because they prevented sinks from overflowing, but because they allowed me to put on deodorant. I'll explain.

Each morning, I took my right hand in my left and hooked its fingers on the edge of the drain hole leaving my thumb outside the counter so that I was gripping the counter's edge. I then picked up my deodorant with my left hand and unscrewed its lid with the same. Holding on to the front of the sink, I slowly backed away from the sink bowing like a royal subject backing away from a throne. Finally, when I was bent fully over and could get my arm no farther from my torso, I applied the deodorant before letting go of the sink and standing back up.

I had not taken a shower at the Best Western, but I knew this reapplication of deodorant would pay hefty dividends by the end of this day, for me and my tent mate.

It had been a terrible night's sleep. I was uncomfortable. The bed was a full instead of a queen, and as a consequence I had no space to extend my right arm without crowding Kirstin off the edge. Compounding this discomfort was an air conditioner so loud and so varying in its tones that when I occasionally did drift off, I dreamt I was inside NASA's Jet Propulsion Laboratories. Not restful.

I awoke about four forty-five and knew immediately that trying to fall back asleep was futile; my mind racing with details of the trip. After my journey to the bathroom for deodorant, and for the next forty-five minutes, I dressed for the day in the dark as quietly as I could to allow Kirstin and Wade a few more minutes' sleep. The list of clothing articles should make it clear what my chief concern was: the sun—ironic, as it was still far from up.

After a bad ankle and shin burn I had received on a lake outing a month earlier, I had decided I would not survive the trip without socks. As icky as it felt to stay in wet socks, it was far preferable to burns and eventual blisters from going without them. The polyester red and blue Texas socks that Wade had given me in the hospital after the stroke seemed the perfect choice; a baby-blue long-sleeve technical fabric T-shirt, which was our crew's uniform at Philmont Scout Ranch; an unintentionally matching light blue "sun gaiter," a stretchy technical fabric tube that, when pulled halfway over my head, covered my ears and entire face and neck below my eyes; long tan fishing pants that were cool, lightweight, quick drying, and that I wore everyday whether kayaking or not; my black plastic—er, *resin*—AFO; sport sandals I had bought years ago and recently modded with a pair of scissors to fit more easily over the AFO; a tan boonie, a floppy, foldable wide-brim hat with a vent around the crown to let out heat; thin, hot-weather camouflage hunting gloves that I had cut the fingertips off of; a yellow and black life jacket; and a clear drybag that hung around my neck by a string that held my phone and wallet. (At my strong urging, Wade had adopted an almost identical get-up, even coincidentally down to the shirt color, so that it almost appeared that we were wearing a team uniform.)

Thus bedecked, it was now after six, which meant our breakfast was ready. I made the first of three trips to the lobby for coffee and breakfast tacos, carrying a cup of burning-hot coffee in my good hand with each round trip. Pandemic rules required no gathering in the dining room, so everything was to-go, and our breakfast order, three sausage-and-egg tacos, had been taken the night before.

At sunrise, we headed just a mile east to the boat ramp. Around the parking lot, Spanish moss hung dreamily from live oaks, and Tejano fishermen tried their luck. It was a fact of life that every time we put in or took out at a bridge, we had to maneuver around fishing lines like a water bug trying to avoid the strands of a spider web.

As we struggled to get the boat strapped to the circus peanut to reach the water, Kirstin walked the two heavy mesh "dunk bags" that held all of our food down the boat ramp, then returned to see what else she could do before we rolled the boat down. "I don't know if this is a good omen or a bad omen," she said, "but I think there's a severed hog's leg right down there by the water." We rolled the boat slowly down the ramp, and sure enough, resting on top of a plastic bag, a hairy black leg that looked torn from its body and smelled about three days old. I could not recreate the scene that produced it. Had a hog been shot, then taken to a boat ramp to be butchered? Had a fisherman been using cut-up hog as bait, and would you leave the hide on for that? Or had an alligator had his way with the pig, and the leg washed up on the ramp and been left high and dry when the river level dropped? It made little sense, but whatever the case, it created an unpleasant obstacle for us before we had even reached the water.

I had learned during the shakedown that steering the boat was a full-time job and that the boat began to go badly off course within five seconds of your hand ever leaving the little plastic tiller. Therefore, I had made the determination that Wade should be in the back and I should be in the front. This would give me the flexibility to do things

THE RIVER NUTS

like take pictures, consult my river notes, and drink with my one good hand instead of that hand always being occupied with steering.

We lifted the boat off the circus peanut and set it broadside to the ramp, nose downstream to the right, and Wade waded in knee-deep and dragged it out to a depth at which it would float. Wade loaded the giant blue dry bag, cart, and red potty bucket and strapped it all down tight for the first of many times with a red mesh tie-down strap. I helped as best I could to jostle the two dunk bags filled with tortillas and peanut butter and tuna and coffee through the oval front hatch and into the hull's nose, what we came to call "the hold."

I kissed Kirstin goodbye. "Thank you, thank you, thank you," I said. "I'll text you with updates." She flashed a genuine smile of happiness for me, one that coexisted with her admitted nervousness.

ÁNDA!

She was genuinely happy I was having an adventure, just as she was genuinely happy that Andrew was having an adventure at the exact same time, but, she said, she would not sleep very well until both of us were back home.

At the truck, Kirstin disengaged my special left-foot accelerator pedal and set it in the back seat, then drove up on the bridge, parked on the highway shoulder over the river, and set the hazard lights flashing.

As she got out to take our picture from above, a state trooper stopped to ask her if everything was okay. Leaping from a bridge into the Nueces at George West would have resulted in a broken ankle at most, but she appreciated his concern nonetheless.

Wade and I sat in the boat, and he pushed us perpendicular out into the river with his paddle as I dropped my prop, got the casserole dish properly oriented, and simultaneously lifted and spastically thrust my right foot forward into it. Meanwhile, Wade was busier than a mosquito in a nudist colony, paddling to turn our nose downstream while trying to drop his own prop and figure out the tiller, all at once.

Beneath the bridge now, as beneath every bridge, were fishermen taking an interest in this strange boat with its strangely dressed and heavily provisioned operators. "What are you fishing for today?" they asked.

"We're not fishing, we're just traveling," I said. "Going from here to the bay."

"*Ánda!*" said one angler. Raised in the Valley, we both knew it was an abbreviation for the exclamation "ándale," and we adopted it as our own for the rest of the trip.

"Love you!" I shouted, and then to the fisherman hastened to add, "Not you, her," pointing above us to the bridge.

TWELVE

GARLAND

"Primordial: existing at or from the beginning of time; primeval."

IMMEDIATELY WE GOT SIDEWAYS AGAIN but finally nosed downstream and fishtailed down the river in a series of over-corrections that the video Kirstin was shooting off the bridge illustrated in excruciating honesty. As I say, it was Wade's first time sitting in back and therefore his first time steering, but over-correcting was easy to do in this weighed-down vessel with a rudder too small for its bulk, and I had over-corrected the entire fifteen miles of our shakedown.

Immediately, we began seeing what the anglers under the bridge were after—alligator gar. Descriptions of this fish always begin with the word *prehistoric*. I have never quite understood that term, because all fish are prehistoric when we consider that history—the recorded story of humanity—is only about six thousand years old, and no form of fish is more recent than that. I think what is actually meant by prehistoric is something like Jurassic or Cretaceous, something you would expect to find only in the fossil record from many millions of years ago and that looks quite different from most other fish, something that looks as if it is still in transition from fish to reptile or from reptile to fish. Though gar are found in most rivers of Texas, surely no river holds more per mile than the Nueces, and none hold bigger specimens. Indeed the world record alligator gar was caught here in the Nueces in 1953: 302 pounds. A gar that size would approach ten feet in length.

The *Atractosteus spatula* is so odd-looking as a whole that one could be forgiven for wondering if, with only a glimpse, it actually was a fish or a reptile. What gives the alligator gar its name is a long, flat head and snout full of sharp teeth. One fishing book describes the eyes as having "an evil truculent glint," which I will allow, though one never held still long enough for me to peer into the windows of its soul.

The gar's body is just as weird, and not gator-like at all. It is tubelike and fat—or should I say muscular—as wide as it is deep, with a flat back and dorsal and anal fins set way back on the body, almost to its tail, which itself is distinct due to its rounded tailfin. Its large scales look like platemail armor and are indeed so hard that American Indians once used them as arrowheads. Their green-gray backs match the water perfectly, but their bellies are white, and their fins and tails are tinted pink.

And while alligator gars were the stars of the show, the smaller needle-nose or "longnose" gar abounded in the same waters. They share many of the same traits, but the species owes its name to a nose three times longer than its head and ten times longer than it is wide.

One reason we saw so many gar was their sheer numbers. But another reason is tied to a curious biological feature. Gar have gills but also, especially during hot weather, surface frequently to gulp air, taking it into a highly vascularized air bladder that serves double duty as a lung. This superpower, unique among fish, allows it to thrive even in water with very low oxygen—in other words, warm, lazy rivers.

So it was they were our constant companions, sometimes swimming under or alongside the boat, sometimes lazily "tailing," with only their pinkish tails and back-set dorsal fins waving hello to us, sometimes violently blowing up the surface so loud as to startle me and send my right arm flailing out of control — a charming neurological feature of my remodeled brain.

~~~~~

All along this stretch, we frequently spied trotlines, thin ropes tied to tree branches that were marked with surveyor's tape. Compact discs marked other trotlines, hanging just above the water from low branches like garish Christmas ornaments. That something once as hi-tech as a 750-megabyte compact disc was now used to mark a trot line was evidence both of the relentless march of technology and the nearly instant obsolescence of the things of the human world. Thirty years earlier, the CD had been the state of the art. Now, it served merely as a more durable form of aluminum foil. By contrast, the thing it was being used to find, the alligator gar, had not lost any value in the 157 million years of its existence. Man's handiwork, God's handiwork.

As a lifelong angler and an occasional hunter, I have never been an animal rights absolutist. But recognizing the self-evident fact that animals do feel, neither have I ever understood the cruelty of things like foot traps and trotlines—the act of impaling or ensnaring something and just letting it suffer until it dies. If you want to catch a fish, be a man—or a woman: catch it and either release it or put it out of its misery quickly.

Above the water, green herons with their dark brown necks and blue-green caps and backs flew low along and across the river, lighting on willows. They look so graceful it was hard to picture them in the depths of their barbarism. When they catch large frogs, they will drown them before swallowing them whole.

But they aren't always so heavy handed. In fact, speaking of fishing, green herons are one of the few species of bird known to fish. Lots of birds wade and spear and gobble fish, but green herons actually use insects, and occasionally other items, as bait. They drop the bug on the water's surface, and as soon as a fish takes the bait, the heron will grab and eat the fish—surely one of the fastest acts of Darwinian karma in the universe.

In a half hour, we saw a creek on our right, and I knew the river notes I had spent so many hours preparing were working. I knew that it was Timon Creek and that we had made it to mile one. At long last, we were discovering the Nueces.

~~~~~~

This unsung, unassuming—almost invisible—river I had crossed at least two hundred times just north of George West was the first river in Texas to appear on a European map. The Portuguese cartographer Diogo Ribeiro drew it in 1527 on a secret Spanish map known as the Padron Real (Royal Census), which is considered the first scientific world map. They called this the Río Escondido, or "Hidden River," due to the fact that its mouth was obscured by what we call Mustang Island.

Before the Spanish arrived and renamed it, as they did nearly everything, the native people of South Texas, whom scholars have lumped together as "Coahuiltecans," called it Chotilapacquen. I searched high and low to try to find a translation for "Chotilapacquen" and came up empty. Finding nothing, I am going to guess that "Chotilapacquen" referred to the stream's most obvious feature and translates roughly as "gar-land."

If Señor Ribeiro had been looking at a live satellite image that year, 1527, instead of his parchment map, he would have seen a strange thing—a small fleet of ships floating very slowly from Cuba to Tampa Bay, Florida, but all the while facing west. This was the Narvaez Expedition, an attempt to sail from Cuba due west across the Gulf of Mexico and establish a port city where Tampico now sits.

But a funny thing happened on the way to the continent—the sailors hit the Gulf Stream, a tremendously powerful current that enters the Gulf below Cuba, swirls clockwise, and exits the Gulf between Cuba and

Florida. They knew nothing of this current. And while they could use the stars to get a rough fix on their north-south position, they could only guess at their east-west position based on how long they had been sailing and how long it took the boat to pass bubbles on the surface of the water. For many days they sailed heading west and assumed they were traveling west. In reality, they were stuck in the Gulf Stream, "sailing" dutifully west but actually drifting due north. The bubbles were passing them, not the other way around. When they came in view of land after what seemed like an appropriate amount of time at sea heading west, they assumed they had landed a few miles from their target, and an expedition set off on foot to find the mouth of the river.

But as you no doubt realize, Tampa Bay, Florida, is a minute or two from Tampico, Mexico. As the crow flies across the Gulf it is exactly one thousand miles. The kindest measurement along the Gulf Coast is 1,500 miles. Having no idea how badly they had screwed the pooch, they kept pressing forward, making one fatal mistake after another. The ships sank off Florida. The Spanish ate their horses, became sick, and were attacked by natives. The fraction that survived made it to the piney woods of Florida's panhandle and, after weeks of hard labor, built four huge rafts as a way to continue searching the coastline for the promised city site, which was a river mouth marked by plentiful palm trees.

The reason we know any of this was that among them was the royal treasurer and the first European to set foot in Texas, Alvar Nuñez Cabeza de Vaca.[3] Starving and dying of thirst, he was dumped off his raft on a stretch of beach just south of Galveston Island, and was promptly enslaved by the locals. It was the beginning of a mind-boggling ten-year journey on foot across the continent to the Pacific, nearly three hundred years before Lewis and Clark.

---

3. In 1519, Spaniard Alonso Álvarez de Pineda mapped the Texas coast. Therefore, if any member of his party landed, they would have been the first European to set foot in Texas, but no account of that expedition survives.

THE RIVER NUTS

One hundred sixty-eight years later, the area was *still* so misunderstood and poorly mapped by Europeans that the French explorer La Salle thought the Nueces was the Mississippi and was on his way to find its mouth when he shipwrecked up the coast near Matagorda Bay, the mouth of the Colorado River, in 1685.

~~~~~~

My river notes were working, but we could not say the same for everything. The first mechanical failure occurred within an hour of launch. After eight trips out, including our fifteen-mile shakedown on the Colorado, Wade's pedal waited until Kirstin was just out of range to begin backing out, unscrewing itself from the crank arm. Using the pliers of a multitool, he tightened it as much as he could, but that led to an unsettling squeak on every turn of the pedal.

With my axle creaking and his pedal squeaking, we briefly considered adopting the trucker CB handles "Creaky and Squeaky," but soon the joke was no longer so funny. The next time he stopped to tighten the pedal, he discovered something disturbing: filings. With each revolution, he was grinding away the inner thread of the crank arm, and we could not figure out why. After all, it had worked fine for six months, including the shakedown, which we did to reveal exactly these kinds of problems in a lower-stakes setting. This was not good for mile one of an eighty-six-mile trip.

Then he glanced at his Fit Bit, which he had brought to gauge our mileage, and its battery was dead. Wanting a little video clip of this stretch of the river, I turned on my GoPro camera, which I had fully charged two weeks earlier, and after three minutes of use, its battery was at 17 percent. We somehow had entered a river version of the Bermuda Triangle.

And now we faced the question we were bound to face sooner or later, though it was sooner rather than later: whence urination? Where—and how—would we wee-wee when the time arrived to make tee-tee? We had brought along an empty apple juice bottle, intending for it to receive the nectar when we were underway, and Wade had successfully used it from the seated position. (Years earlier, when the boys and I had brought a similar bottle along on rafting trips, we had adopted the slogan, "Do *not* drink the apple juice.") I, however, concluded that I needed to get out of the boat for neuromuscular reasons at roughly the same intervals dictated by my urinary tract, and so I should just combine activities, bearing weight through my right leg and hip to relieve spasticity and cramping and emptying my bladder while I was at it.

My eyes searched both banks for an easy spot to land, and there was not much to choose from, most of the bank being lined with willow branches that overhung the water. When I did spot a muddy beach river-left, I asked Wade to steer us to it. On arrival, he swung his legs over the kayak's edge and gamely slid into the brown opaque water to hold the boat still. My choice of a partner on this trip was already paying dividends; I dearly loved this man.

Then it was my turn. Pushing down on my seat with my left arm, I scooched to the side edge of my black mesh seat, grabbed my right leg by the AFO, and pulled it to join my left, socks, sandals, and brace all in the drink. We were thigh-high in Nehi. The bottom was soft and the mud gave way easily under my weight, so Wade grabbed my arm and steadied me. "All right... here goes nothing," I said, jerking the zipper down with my left hand and freeing Willy, as Wade averted his eyes but continued holding onto the belt of the life jacket. Fifteen seconds. Thirty seconds. A minute. No sound of liquid hitting liquid. "Dude," Wade said at last, "what's up? Stage fright?"

Stage fright was a well-established phenomenon among men in public restrooms in which they are incapable of going when others are waiting for them and watching them. "Nah," I said, "it just sometimes takes awhile." Truthfully, it was a combination of three things: First was age—even when I was all by myself and sitting down, it could take a bit to relax all the right muscles and mentally let go the bladder; I assumed this was the prostate enlargement nearly universal in men in their late forties and fifties. Second was the stroke, which greatly complicated the business of relaxation, especially on a sloping surface, and especially in the crazy-soft mud into which we now were both sinking. And third, stage fright.

At length I concluded that if I was to ever go, I needed to be on dry, level ground, and yes, to be alone so that I could do the "Michael Jordan thing." The Michael Jordan thing was a visualization exercise that I went through every time I was having trouble peeing, and, with apologies to Michael Jordan, it involves a slow-motion replay of MJ dunking from the free-throw line to the chorus of R. Kelly's "I Believe I Can Fly," which is probably a direct clip from the movie *Space Jam*. I don't know how it got started. I don't know why it works. I just know it does, and I long ago stopped questioning it.

So with Wade going ahead of me and offering a hand, I stumbled and slid ashore and with a few more steps was on solid dry ground, and now I saw the problem with the spot I had picked for us to land. Cattle hoof prints on shore told the story of a dozen cows and bulls who regularly made their way down to the water right here for a drink. Below the water's surface, they had churned up the once-hard bottom into workable clay. I side-stepped my way around a low-hanging live oak branch, faced away from Wade, who was enjoying his first cigarette of the trip, and distributed my weight evenly. "I believe I can fly . . . I believe I can touch *mmm-hmm*, I think about it *mmm-mmm-mmm-mmmm*" . . . Right on cue, I was right with the world, and in two more minutes, we were back on the water and pedaling downriver.

~~~

After about three hours, at mile six, we came to our first real landmark, a one-lane bridge built primarily of railroad ties. It was one we had scouted a week earlier and determined there was no access to the river.

It ran past a 150-year-old live oak that had received a historical marker saying that this was the first gathering spot in Live Oak County.

At about noon, around mile eleven, the character of the river began to change, widening and slowing as we approached the head of Lake Corpus Christi. We began encountering long islands, oxbow lakes, and large peninsulas. And the orange duct tape Ian had wrapped the boat in was already paying off, as motorboats encountering us suddenly at bends in the river throttled down as they spotted us and drifted slowly past. "What are y'all catching today?" they would ask.

"Not fishing, just traveling," one or the other of us would reply, always eliciting a look of confusion in the other boat, followed by a polite smile and wave goodbye.

I had, on my laminated cards, noted that when we passed a subdivision that was on an island, we should stay to the right to take the shortest path or "inside track" along the river channel that was now wide and riddled with confusing peninsulas that could lead us wastefully into backwaters. Just then we passed a man on shore. "'Scuse me," I said, "is this subdivision on an island?"

"No," the man answered, with a confused expression.

"OK, thanks," I said.

"Have a good one," Wade added, ever friendly.

Skeptical, I turned on my phone and opened the Find My iPhone app, which produced a map with a pulsating dot showing our precise location. I zoomed in as close as I could get, and sure enough, we had just passed the subdivision on an island. How someone could live on an island and not know it remains something of a mystery to me, but I suppose he had never noticed that he had to cross a short bridge every time he came home or left his neighborhood. An island, after all, is something in the South Pacific with palm trees and white-sand beaches.

We took a hard right at the next island as my notes instructed but soon found ourselves in less than four inches of water. All my strategizing about keeping the inside track and saving time had backfired, and now we had to backtrack to return to the main channel. Some minutes later, sadder but wiser, we were back on track.

Soon the river widened out even more and we found ourselves amidst vast stands of snags, the branchless remnants of dead trees protruding above the water. Perhaps they once formed a riparian forest on the stream bank before the river was dammed a century ago and the lake it created backed up to flood this area. Perhaps they sprang to life when the lake went down and this became dry land. Whatever the case, we now chose our line of travel carefully so as to not become trapped by the hundreds of gray snags nor to catch a submerged log with a prop.

A bridge that carried Highway 534 over the river signaled that we had gone 16.8 miles. By the time we had cranked beneath a railroad bridge, we were at 17.5. The wide river wound to the south, and the sun found a break in the clouds low in the sky to our right and lit the day in golden-hour splendor. The clouds through which it had found a break stretched across the sky, and before us, in the east, grew darker and rose up along the coast in towering charcoal thunderheads. A distant rumbling rolled across the land intermittently, and we pedaled a little faster.

On our left now was an odd grouping of buildings that I assumed comprised a low-rent church camp of some kind, owing to the large cross standing near the water. Then two men rolled even with us in a golf cart. "What are you all catching?" the driver called out.

"We're not fishing, we're just traveling," said Wade.

"Where ya going?"

"Put in at George West and are headed to the bay," Wade answered.

"What the shit?!" said a bearded man in the cart's passenger seat, who I noticed was holding a flask. Well, I thought, I guess it's not a church camp after all.

Along with "*ánda!*" "What the shit?!" became another favored saying of the voyage for us. Spoken like a scholar and a gentleman. What the shit, indeed, my good sir, what the shit . . . indeed.

The driver of the golf cart told us about a property he owned on the lake not too far away, Lagarto—something or other—and said we were welcome to stay there if we wanted to. It was a kind offer, the first of several on the trip. I think there is something inside people in general that wants to support the adventures of others. By participating in some small way, they are getting a little bit of adventure for themselves. We shouted our thanks and told him we might take him up on it, but the description of what to look for from the water was bewildering, we were ready to stop for the day, and our planned stop was dead ahead.

The clouds to our immediate northeast were growing darker by the moment, and the rumbling was getting closer. We had to land as soon as possible. We ran ashore on an island smaller than my front yard at the head of the lake. The large island I had seen on the map and planned for us to camp on was still a thousand yards away, but this one would do nicely under the circumstances.

Wade pulled the boat up on dry ground, and I tied the bow handle to a large orange plastic screw I had brought as a ground anchor. Back upriver, a lightning bolt lit up the sky, and the near immediate crack told us that it had struck less than a quarter mile away.

Now it began to rain, not mist or sprinkle, but large pelting drops, the kind that make you wince a little when they hit you. And I realized a strategic error. That morning, at my suggestion, we had put the tent at the bottom of the dry bag. I had suggested this because under normal conditions I would have wanted to get to my stool first, then to the duffle bag that held ninety percent of our gear, then to the tent, when we were finally ready to set it up. These were not normal conditions. The tent setup now was urgent, so we grabbed the dry bag, turned it upside down, and shook it out into the driving rain. This ensured that everything we had put in the dry bag now was soaked, day one.

As I said, the island was small, and so the options for setting up the tent were few and obvious. Clearing a stick and a rock off the grassy flat, I tried my best to help spread the tent out and shake the shock-cord poles into their straight configuration, but before long I was only in the way. Wade wrestled the poles into their hooks as I tried to hold one at the corners so he could raise and get the other side onto its peg.

But now gale-force winds hit the tiny island, inverting the tent as Wade, like Buster Keaton, continued the Sisiphean chore of getting both ends of the poles attached so that the tent would finally assume its domed shape.

Meanwhile, I focused on damage control, unzipping the door and throwing the duffle in, both to get it out of the rain and to add weight to the tent so it wouldn't blow into the lake like a box kite. I followed the duffle into the tent and in a slow roll collapsed to the ground. The tent was definitely not blowing into the lake now.

In a minute that must have seemed to Wade like an hour, he climbed into the tent too, panting, lowered the rain fly, and zipped the door closed, both of us laughing in nervous disbelief at the Weather Channel special exploding all around us.

In twenty minutes, the rain let up, and the wind died to nothing. It was as if we had been hit by a hurricane that was exactly one mile across. Before Wade bedded down for the night, he walked back to the boat, retrieved the little yellow plastic Dickie's Barbecue cup we had used to bail the boat's cockpits, and used it to bail the tent's floor.

Overnight, the rain came again, pelting the tent like machine-gun fire, but the rainfly did its job, and we were dry, if a tad sticky.

We had pedaled twenty miles in about nine hours. With that, I was pleased. But I knew that tomorrow would likely be the hardest day of the trip.

Wade between storms at the head of Lake Corpus Christi.

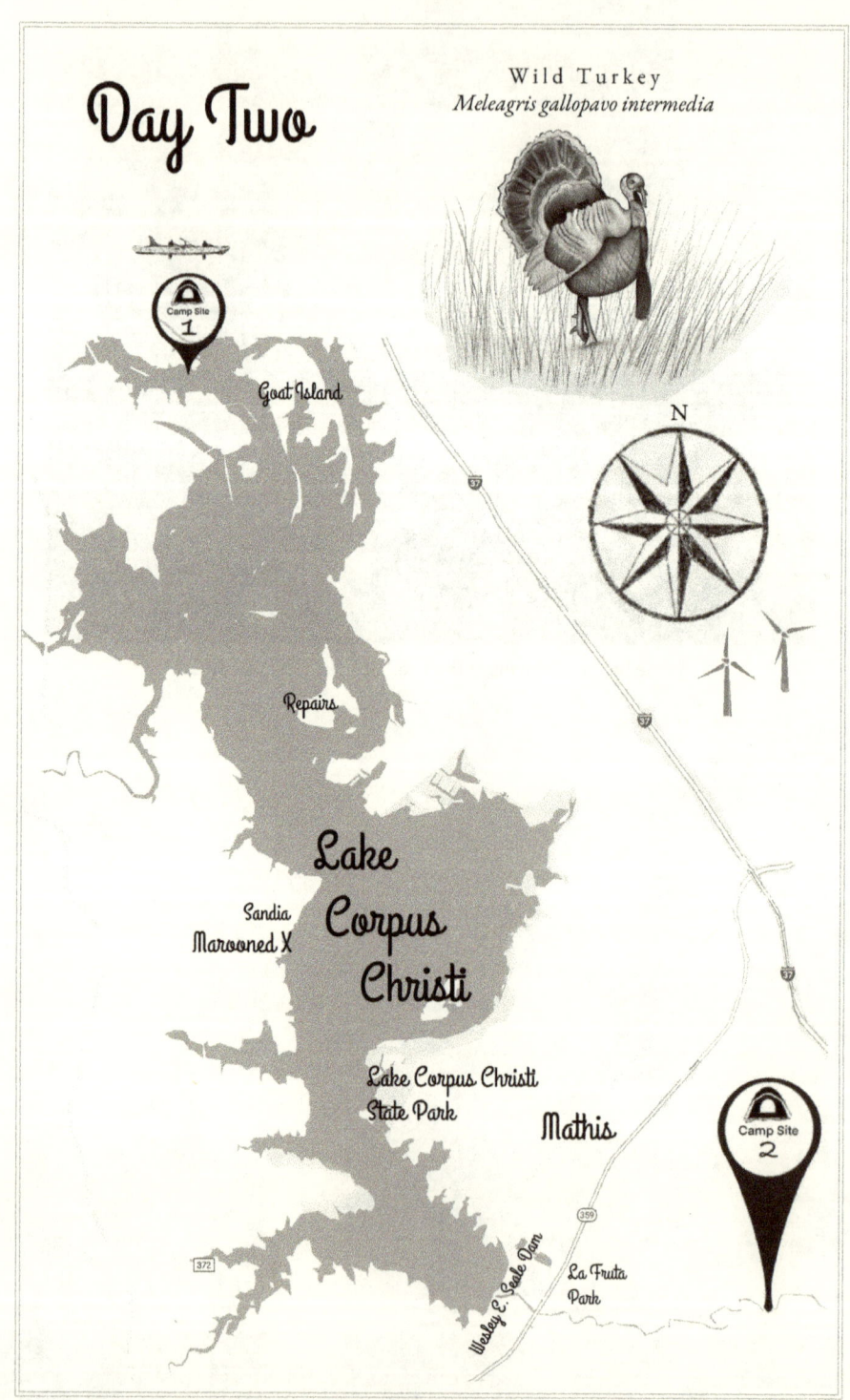

THIRTEEN

A DAMMED SHAME

"The wind shows us how close to the edge we are."
—JOAN DIDEON

FIRST LIGHT OF DAY TWO brought an explosion of pink in the clouds over the lake to our southeast. The majestic vista shifted from bright pink to pale pink and, as the sun showed itself just south of the large island to our east, to gold, the effect doubled as whatever changed above us in the sky changed before us in the water. As I stood there chewing a protein bar and chasing it with a tiny bottle of 5-Hour Energy, I looked at the clouds. This is why I do it, I thought.

I had set up the red five-gallon bucket affixed with the black plastic toilet seat near the island's lone tree, a sorry old shrub that offered little cover but perhaps veiled my silhouette to those who might have been boating into the lake from the river. I dug a cat hole in the sandy mud, placed the bottomless bucket over the hole, then dropped the fishing pants down, pulling them over the AFO, and carefully lowered myself to the seat, which only shifted a little under its new load. With a soft chuckle, I thought of the journey this device had made.

I had bought the potty bucket as I was preparing for our first raft trip, not knowing how else the boys and I would evacuate our bowels in the middle of a river with no guarantee of being able to get to shore. Of course, there's no such thing as digging a cat hole on a wooden raft, so my solution was to fill the bucket about a quarter with kitty litter, keeping with the cat theme.

When we made a Labor Day trip up Lady Bird Lake in downtown Austin, we brought the bucket and kitty litter along, and whensoever one of us heard the call of nature—only No. 1 that day—we would wrap a beach towel around our waist, drop our swim trunks, sit on the bucket, and relax serenely as passing boaters, none the wiser, waved at us and made cheerful conversation. I would gamely field their questions about the raft whilst urinating to my heart's content. A splendid system, no Michael Jordan thing even necessary.

I knew this would be a difficult day, as we had to traverse the entire fifteen-mile north-to-south length of the twenty-thousand-acre reservoir. In the sweep of history, this stretch of the Nueces had been thus for only the last few moments.

In January 1929, the construction of La Fruta Dam across the Nueces formed a reservoir called Lake Lovenskiold, after Corpus Christi's mayor at the time. In what must be a record of some kind, the dam lasted just ten months, failing in November of that same year, less than a month after the stock market did the same. By 1935, FDR's New Deal was in full swing, and the dam was rebuilt. The improved structure was called Mathis Dam for the nearest town, and the reconstituted reservoir was named Lake Corpus Christi.

But by the Forties, so much silt was filling the lake that it was significantly reducing its capacity. A new dam was proposed to create a larger lake, which landowners in the proposed flood pool naturally opposed and delayed with lawsuits for more than a decade. But you can't fight city hall, or the water supply district, which won a key court decision clearing the way for a new seventy-five-foot earthen dam, completed in 1958. It is named Wesley E. Seale Dam (no relation).

FDR's old Mathis Dam still stands at the bottom of Lake Corpus Christi. But to this day, locals often refer to it as Lake Mathis because that is the largest town of the many along its lengthy shore, including Swinney Switch (named for a railroad switch station), Dinero, Sandia, Lagarto, and Lake City.

Speaking of Swinney Switch, I switched to the back seat that morning as part of a larger strategy to conserve the boat's working parts and make it as far down the river as possible. With Wade's pedal coming loose, I thought we would be better off if I was in the back where I could crank with maximum power and steer, and he could paddle from the front if need be. This was the only way that both of us could have both power and steerage, a critical factor in the event that either of us went overboard.

The sun had made a spectacular appearance at sunrise, but by the time we shoved off it was already behind clouds, and soon enough, the rain started once again, and we began cycling back and forth for the rest of the trip between soaked to the bone and merely damp. I wondered if we would ever be truly dry again.

We were headed to Sunrise Beach, a rather glamorous name for an RV park run by the city of Corpus Christi, which sat at the north end of the dam fifteen miles to our south. There, we would meet my brother Erren, who was driving his pickup truck three hours from McAllen to help us take the 'yak four miles out to the highway, around the dam, and back to the river below the lake. I had given him a best estimate of four o'clock that afternoon for our rendezvous.

We passed to the south of a large island, which locals called Goat Island, at the head of the vast lake, but we did not pass close enough to confirm the presence of the ruminants.

I had planned to bear left now and follow the lake's shoreline for safety's sake, but I quickly abandoned that plan, not because the points we needed to round looked too distant but because they looked so close and attainable, and it seemed like a waste of valuable time and energy to go anywhere but straight to the next point. After all, the life jacket was clipped, the water was calm, and the boat felt steady.

About a mile into the lake, Wade's right pedal thunked into the floor of his cockpit. It had made its final revolution, and no amount of body English or wishful thinking would hold it in place. "Well shit," I said. We suspected this moment was inevitable but had hoped that perhaps it wouldn't come at the farthest possible spot from land. But the universe is fickle, and no sooner do you begin celebrating some turn of good fortune and start questioning whether Murphy's Law really exists, than it humbles you with something like this. Wade proceeded to push the crank arm directly with his foot, and when that became ineffective began using his arms to turn the cranks.

No matter how many times I told him to chill, and that I was happy to do this part, and that he would get his turn when it was time to pitch camp, he would, within five minutes, be back to turning those crank arms by some weird method. He was constitutionally incapable of chilling out, a virtue that in general served us well and for which I was ultimately grateful. Subconsciously, that conscientiousness was probably among the chief reasons I approached him about doing the trip in the first place.

Then I noticed something. Just as Wade's right pedal had begun backing out of its hole yesterday, now my pedal was doing the same. What fresh hell was this? And now the whole trip flashed before my eyes and my boundless optimism took an excruciating punch to the crotch. I kept a close eye on the joint, inspecting it every minute or so. From the front seat, Wade turned 180 degrees and with the multi-tool's pliers gently turned it back in. Five minutes later, it was backing out again. It seemed too much of a coincidence that my right pedal was doing the exact same thing his right pedal had done the day before. And now Wade made a deeply frustrating discovery, one that at this remove seems almost too obvious to put in print: on both drives, the crank arms were marked left and right, and both drives had them reversed.

For the last twenty-four hours I had been bemoaning "cheap-ass Chinese pot metal" for his drive's pedal falling apart when it actually was user error during assembly on that excited night back in December when I had screwed all of this together, apparently facing the back of the boat instead of the front. But why, in the name of Engelbert Humperdinck, did it all work perfectly for six months, including on our fifteen-mile shakedown, only to fail now when the stakes were highest?

Now that we had figured out the root of the problem, we would not make the same mistake as yesterday by continuing to tighten the pedal and then grinding the threads to metallic dust. We had to land and fix the problem.

Fortunately, straight ahead was another very large, treed island where we had planned to land anyway. Large wooden NO TRESPASSING signs ringed the island's perimeter, but we were undeterred, as we now had both mechanical emergencies and biological urgencies to tend: We were overdue for a stretch to straighten our aching bodies and decompress the tissue around our tailbones. We both had to pee. For neuromuscular reasons, I needed to stand and bear weight through my right hip and leg. And Wade was jonesing for a cigarette, as he voluntarily had refrained from smoking whenever we were underway. Our to-do list was getting long.

After we had landed and all of those biological errands had been run, we set upon the boat, savaging every part with the multi-tool pliers and Allen wrenches of all sizes. First, we switched the left and right crank arms on both drives, then tightened the axles, then tightened the props. Because we switched the crank arms, we had to switch the casserole dish to my new right pedal.

Because one of Wade's crank arms had been irreparably stripped of the interior threads that held in the pedal, we took a bolt, brought along as a spare for the casserole dish mount, and tightened it with a wing nut through the hole where the pedal once fit. A bolt for a pedal was not great, as it concentrated all of the pressure of each revolution on the arch of Wade's left foot, but it was a huge improvement over nothing at all. Finally, we tightened the seats, put the tools back in their hatch under my seat, and screwed the hatch cover back on tight.

I squeezed a tuna salad packet onto a tortilla and refilled my LifeStraw-fitted water bottle from the lake.

After the lengthy but productive pit stop, we shoved back into deep water, dropped the props, and began cranking to the south as, of course, the rain started again. We cleared the next point around noon, marking mile twenty-six. We had almost completed a marathon, which I had never run but which Wade had run many times. One of his favorite pictures of himself is the one in which he's standing at the finish line of Austin's marathon, covered in sweat and holding a lit cigarette.

We cleared the peninsula on our left, and in another half hour had passed another point on our right, one with palm trees and lots of parallel piers. I studied our position relative to those palms and piers to try and gauge our progress.

Now I began noticing two things at once. The waves had kicked up, and we were beginning to rock. My left hand was busy, as I grasped my seat bottom, then adjusted the tiller, then quickly grasped my seat bottom again before the next roll.

The other thing I noticed was that the boat kept turning to our left, even though I held the rudder right. I learned this was a principle known as *weathervaning*. The wind wanted to follow the path of least resistance around the kayak, and that meant turning us into itself. The exact same principle that makes the pointy bow shape good for slicing through the water when we were providing the power was the principle that pushed us into a backward-facing position when the wind was in charge. Likewise, whenever we stopped pedaling or paddling on the river, the current would slowly turn us around and push us stern-first downstream.

Each time the wind weathervaned us, Providence gave us a splendid visual aid, just in case we had not understood the concept: directly before us, perhaps a mile away, enormous white wind-farm windmills were turning briskly, and their heading was exactly ours.

It was Cabeza de Vaca all over again—facing one way and traveling another. He had left Cuba facing west toward Mexico, and after the appropriate number of days sailing, landed in Florida, some thousand miles from his intended destination. We were on pace for a similar result if we didn't figure this out.

We studied the shore to which we had been heading for quite a while, and despite our continuous cranking, we were not convinced we were actually gaining on it. We had been heading that way for so long and the chop was now so rough that I had decided we should land at the nearest point, call Erren, and have him pick us up there instead of at Sunrise Beach.

"Dude," I said from the rear seat, "which is closer, that shore straight ahead or that point we passed back on the right, the one with the palm trees?"

Wade craned his head to look back over his right shoulder. "Definitely that one," he said, pointing behind us.

This wasn't the plan, and it hurt me to have wasted the last hour of pedaling, but nature always gets the last word, and if we didn't have enough sense to get to shore right then, Wade's words, "Definitely that one," might be his last. We had to cut our losses. If we committed the logical fallacy of "sunk costs" and continued to pursue a losing proposition because of the investment we had already made, we verily would put the "sunk" in "sunk costs."

For a moment, I let the wind have its way and just push us backward, but soon I could tell that it would not push us to the closest point on the shore, nor even to a house, but rather would strand us on an unpopulated shore, and one with a steep bank for good measure. We had to steer, which meant we had to turn around and start cranking again. As we turned, waves started breaking over the side of the boat, and although I was bailing, by now there was so much water in my cockpit it looked like I was sitting in a bathtub. "All I need is a bottle of Epsom salts and a rubber ducky," I said, trying hard to lighten the mood a bit. This would have been an ideal situation in which to pull the scupper plugs, and let water out of the cockpit, but that option never occurred to me as I single-mindedly pedaled and, with my one good hand, rapidly alternated between bailing and adjusting the tiller, to keep our heading toward the closest point on shore.

As we approached land, we saw two fishermen sitting on a private dock. *"Hey . . . we're in trouble!"* I yelled. *"Can we come ashore?"* They said sure and kept on fishing as we maneuvered beneath the dock they were sitting on. The similarities to Cabeza de Vaca's misfortunes did not end with being blown off course. For just as his log raft was hurled ashore by an angry surf near Galveston Island, our vessel now landed hard amidst virtual breakers coming off the lake. I had not stood for several hours, and as the waves pounded the muddy bank, I lost my footing immediately and fell backward into the shallow water. After I struggled to my feet, Wade hauled the boat onto dry ground.

Happily, the similarities to the Spanish expedition *did* end there, because instead of being enslaved and abused for four years by the native population, we were greeted warmly by the homeowner, who had taken note of his newly acquired castaways and made his way down from his house to the water. David, a retired navy man, was a friendly sort and commiserated that he had been through a similar ordeal when he and his son were on the lake the previous spring.

I texted Erren: "Change of plans: marooned ourselves at 222 S. Vista Drive, Sandia." Thankfully, he had decided to hit the road early that morning and, as was his habit, take the scenic route through small towns, photographing unsung architectural gems along the way. This meant he was very near.

The fishermen, David's son and son-in-law, now came down off the pier and helped Wade roll the boat up a long, low, grassy hill to the road. We sat in the shade and waited for Erren. In ten minutes, his gray Toyota Tundra was pulling in front of the kayak, and we were lifting it into his bed and ratcheting it down. I had not seen him in many months, and I wanted to hug him, but coronavirus had made such habitual shows of affection awkward if not an outright no-no. Plus, I was damp, and hot, and smelled terrible, and so did not hug him in keeping with the Golden Rule. I trusted that he was smiling under his Dia de los Muertos face mask as I hoped he knew I was smiling under my baby-blue sun gaiter.

FOURTEEN

JUST WANNA GET DOWN

"But when I came, alas, to wive,
With hey, ho, the wind and the rain,
By swaggering could I never thrive,
For the rain it raineth every day."

—WILLIAM SHAKESPEARE,
"TWELFTH NIGHT," ACT 5, SCENE 1

THOUGHTFULLY, ERREN HAD BOUGHT a couple of cold bottles of water at his last gas stop, and Wade and I pulled off our sun gaiters and drank eagerly as I trained the AC vents on my face and Erren navigated a series of two-lane highways to get us to the dam at the south end of the lake.

We stopped at a tackle store near the dam for a Dr Pepper and to ask about passage to the water. The couple working at the counter warned us against trying to take the truck down to the water on the other side of the bridge. "It's muddy over there," said the man, "and people who drive back up in there tend to fall off the road." Instead, he suggested we put in at La Fruta Park just a block or so farther down river. We drove to La Fruta, and, like Wally World, the park was closed, presumably due to COVID-19. ("Sorry, folks! The moose out front shoulda told ya!") So we went back to the store and pleaded with the couple to let us roll the boat to the water behind their store.

"No," he said with a pleasant smile. "You can put in on the other side of the bridge."

"But . . . you just told me ten minutes ago that it was muddy and dangerous," I said, "that people fall off the road."

"Yep," the man said, then spoke nothing more. His wife looked on in complicit silence. It was clear that neither were going to do johnny jack rat crap to help us, lifelong dream or not. I turned silently and limped out of the store.

Navy David of Sandia had increased our faith in humanity, and this couple just took it right back to neutral. All we wanted was to get back to the river. It reminded me of an issue rarely raised in debates about the border wall along the Rio Grande: building a wall solid enough to keep humans out also must be solid enough to keep wildlife, American wildlife, that is, away from the Rio Grande, water it desperately needs in arid South Texas. The Wildlands Network puts it this way: "These walls, euphemistically referred to as 'replacement fencing,' are 30 feet high and made of six-inch diameter steel beams (known as bollards) with barely four-inch wide gaps between the bollards, inhibiting all wildlife movement for any creature larger than a cottontail rabbit." Even west of El Paso, where the Rio Grande no longer demarcates the border, the wall has devastating effects on wildlife because it disrupts natural migratory routes, such as cutting off jaguars in the United States from their breeding grounds in Mexico. Sometimes a wolf or a deer—or a human—just needs to get to a river. It's pretty basic.

Fortunately, we had something javelinas and ocelots and sonoran pronghorn antelope do not have, and that is satellite imagery. Back south over the bridge, we resolved to put in at a place we had scouted the previous weekend—difficult but at least possible. We parked the truck in a gravel lot, and I decided to change into dry clothes. Not knowing exactly how to do that, I set my stool down next to the truck, and Erren held a beach towel between me and the fence that surrounded the dam, the fence on which were mounted multiple signs that informed us that our movements were being captured on security cameras.

When I was finally dressed again, we unloaded the 'yak, lifting it over the thigh-high steel cable that demarcated the parking lot, and ratchet-strapping it to the circus peanut. Erren and Wade began rolling it along the grassy cut a quarter-mile to the river as I hobbled along behind them, trying to keep up. When we reached the river, a concrete ramp led down to the water, but it was narrow and clearly meant only for foot traffic. With a chain-link fence flush with the left side of the ramp, even the kayak was nearly too wide for it.

And it was not only narrow but steep. We therefore had to divest the boat of all its extra weight—pedal drives, the blue drybag, the white mesh dunk bags holding our food. Then, with Erren spotting the front of the boat on the downhill side, Wade fastened a red tie-down strap to the stern handle. This allowed him to stand up straight and even lean backward while lowering the boat down the steep ramp with baby steps. I followed behind them carrying one of the drives down the ramp as my token contribution to the effort.

After Erren had made several more trips up and down the ramp for gear, he stood at the top of the high bank snapping pictures, then moved off into the trees and back toward his truck. I had asked him to take a few pictures of us from the nearby bridge under which we would pass in about ten minutes.

Between the dam and the bridge a few hundred yards downriver, locals were fishing for gar, of course. One young Tejano caught a thirty-incher just as we passed him. "No hook!" he shouted to us, waving. Wade and I stared, wondering how that was possible. Seems he had simply cast a gauze bandage and a weight into the water, and the fish bit down on the cotton and couldn't get its teeth free. Just as he held the muscular beast aloft to show us, it writhed violently, whipping back and forth, and slapped him hard in the face as its final act in life. It didn't slap his smile off, though.

Now we pedaled beneath the highway bridge and saw Erren, good to his word, snapping pictures with his camera. (One of these is this book's cover.) "Thanks again!" we called up to him. As the bridge disappeared behind us, it once again began to rain. Thank heavens I had taken those ten minutes to change into dry clothes.

Around a bend, we passed a young Mexican American couple pedaling side by side upriver in a paddle boat, smiling serenely under an umbrella, in no hurry. That's living, I thought to myself. They've figured it out.

A mile or so later, we saw three men in their twenties on a fishing platform halfway up a steep bank on our right. "What are you catching?" one shouted.

"We're not fishing, just traveling," I said.

"How far are you going?" he asked.

"To the bay," said Wade.

"Oh wow. That's about three days," he said. He was exactly right. We stopped pedaling and drifted. His was the first and only comment we ever heard that implied that someone had made this trip before, though of course many must have. "So you're just camping or what?"

"Yeah, just finding islands or whatever along the way," I said.

"If you go about twenty more minutes, on your right you're gonna see a spot right before a rock wall where we cleared out some trees and built a camp. You can stay there if you want."

"Oh, that would be great!" I said. "Thanks so much!"

In fifteen minutes, we came to a place that matched his description. Wade pulled the kayak onto a grassy bank, and I tied its bow handle to a PVC pipe buried in the ground, probably as a rod holder, and then tied the stern handle to another. We pitched the tent ten feet from the river under large oaks. The spot even had a canvas camp chair and a hammock. It all seemed too good to be true at the end of such a long, harrowing day. It was the perfect camp, and one we would never have dared to occupy without the invitation. In fact, even though it matched the description, it took several minutes before we convinced each other that this really was the spot he described, and that the real landowner was not going to come charging down to the water and hold a rifle on us.

We began setting up to distant thunder. As Wade started to pitch the tent, a loud sound almost like barking came from just feet away. With another round of barks, I knew it was an owl roosting almost directly overhead, though we could not see it. Next, wild turkeys began calling from an unseen position a little past the bend in the river, sounding just like the stick-and-slate call I had used on the few occasions I had tried to bow-hunt turkey.

Being wet for so long and now almost cold, I thought beef stew might be just the meal for the occasion. So I cut open two bags of Omeals that our friend Ed thoughtfully had delivered to the house a few days before we left. They were ingenious high-end meals perfect for campers with easy access to water. For each meal, we cut the outer bag open, removed the food bag and the heating element bag that is activated by oxygen, similar to the hand warmers and toe warmers I had used before on cold campouts. I filled the bags one-third with river water, then cut open the heating element bag, dumped it in, put the food bag in, and sealed the outer bag up. Within twenty seconds, the river water was simmering, and within thirty seconds it was at a violent boil, a vent hole manufactured in the top of the bag letting off steam like a tiny locomotive. Fifteen minutes later, we were eating pipin'-hot vegetable-and-beef stew out of our plastic bowls in the rain, Wade standing next to the tent, me making myself at home in the dirty, wet red canvas camp chair.

~~~

Evening fell with the tap-tap-tap of light rain coming and going on our tent. Throughout the night, the owls kept up their call and response, and soon I knew they were barred owls, one a tenor, the other, on the other side of the river, an alto. Each one would recite a two-line poem: a question followed by an answer, "Who cooks for you? You cook for you." And then the other would repeat the question and the answer: "Who cooks for you? You cook for you." This went on seemingly for hours into the night. "Who cooks for you? You cook for you. Who cooks for you? You cook for you." At one point, I thought about bursting out of tent: "Look! I know the question of who cooks for whom is an important one. Establishing a clear understanding of the division of labor is crucial to any successful relationship. I get that! Maybe this week, you, sir, the one above me, can do the cooking for both of you, and you—across the river—you can clean up. How does that sound? Actually, I don't hear any disagreement! Both of you have been crystal clear that the other one should cook for themselves. Why are we still talking about this?! Can we can all get a little friggin' shut-eye now?!"

Actually, I didn't mind their call-and-response in the least; in fact, I loved it.

For my money, owls are among the finest things in life. Twenty-some years prior, I had become familiar with the small screech owls that took up residence in our neighborhood, intermittently living in the owl house the boys and I had built for them, on the rare occasions that squirrels and starlings relinquished it. We occasionally spied a great horned owl in the neighborhood as well, when the bare hackberry trees of December revealed what looked like a cat perched on their highest branches. And most winter nights, Kirstin and I could hear the "who-who . . . who-who" of the great horned owls in the distance as we lay in bed.

But there is something special about the barred owl. It turns out that the Nueces River is at the southernmost edge of their vast North American range, which stretches from Texas and Florida north to Ontario and west to the Great Plains. They can live more than twenty years, but they never go more than six miles from where they were born. Through the last century, they worked their way across Canada to the Pacific and now have taken up residence with their closest relatives, spotted owls, with whom they are hybridizing, much as the Coahuiltecans hybridized away their distinctive genes and culture with the arrival of the Spanish in Texas.

Besides turkeys and owls, there were two other opera stars that night: frogs, which surrounded our tent on all sides and sang loudly throughout the night, and of course the distant chorus of yipping coyote pups, a standard feature of any night outdoors in North America.

We reckoned we had reached about mile thirty-six, and thus were closing on the halfway point.

FIFTEEN

SCRAPING BY

"Sight is a faculty, but seeing is an art."
—ANONYMOUS

WE HEADED OUT ON DAY THREE in a steady rain, which I found peaceful. The surface of the river, normally as smooth as glass, was pockmarked with each drop, their ripples intersecting at all angles, as if the river was simmering. Birds continued to fly along and across the river, not the least bit intimidated by the rain. Thunder rumbled in the distance, so far away that we felt it in our chests more than heard it.

Our choice of early June was paying dividends, as we were not cold even soaked to the bone. We had brought along rain suits, stuffed in the front hatch for quick access, but never once did we reach for them. The scene was one of peaceful surrender dictated by the intersection of nature and our schedules. While in other times we might have sat in the tent and waited out the storm, by day three we already were battle-hardened by a storm far worse than this that had pummeled us as Wade struggled to set up the tent on night one, and by the rain that soaked us while we were on the lake the next morning, and by the rain that rinsed us off yet again as we pulled into the camp last night. We were now way beyond caring about being wet. Pulling on wet socks every morning and wading knee deep to float the boat before taking our seats had become routine. Wet all the time. Might as well lean in.

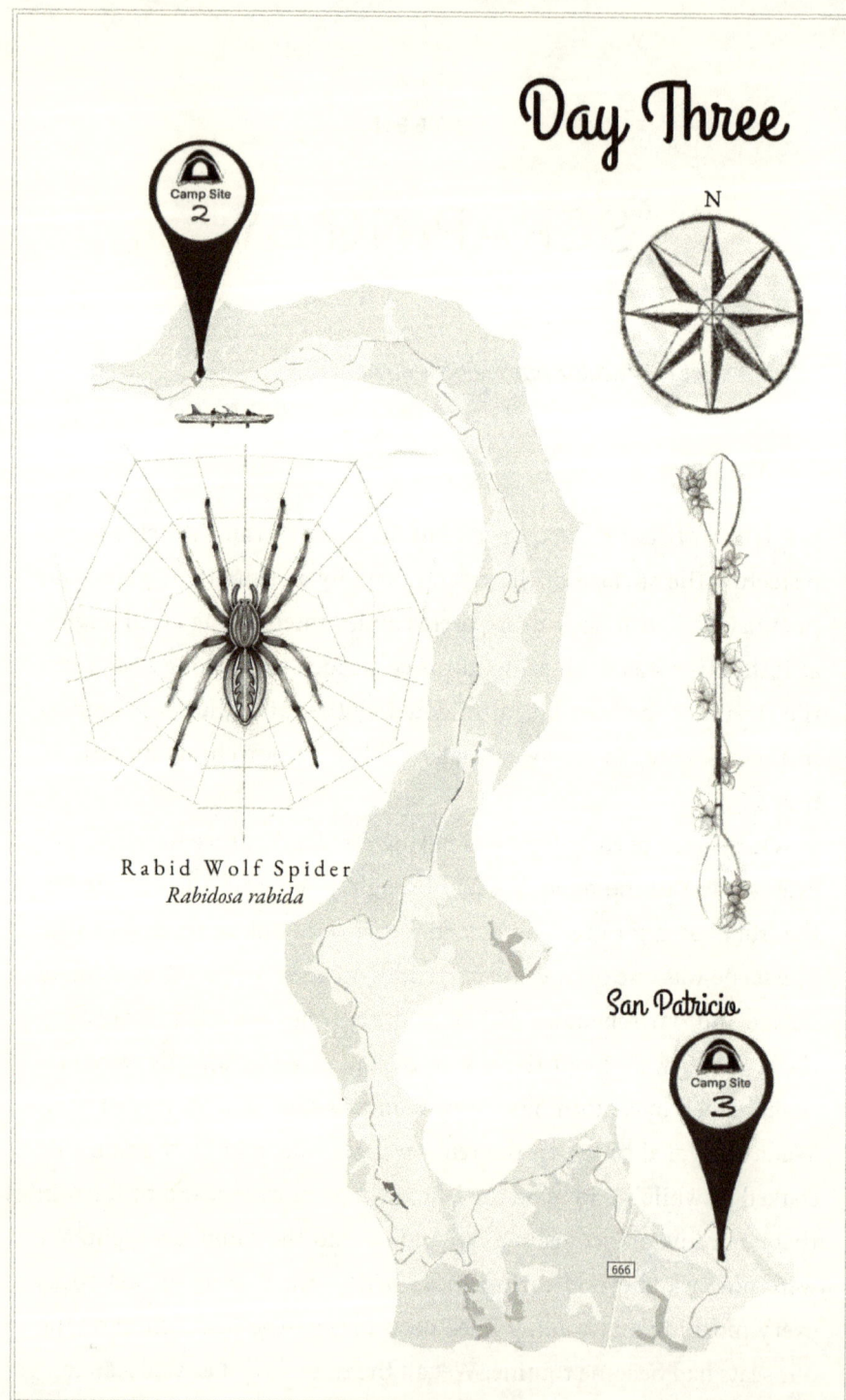

SCRAPING BY

Peaceful as the rain was, I watched the river level closely for any sign of rapid rise or swift-water injections from creeks or draws. I would not be on guard thus did I not live in Central Texas, where deadly flash floods are at least an annual occurrence, and where the public service slogan "Turn Around, Don't Drown" is known to all. Nor would I be so vigilant had we not very nearly lost the boat two weeks earlier on a fast-flowing Colorado, flush with rain from the night before.

After a half hour or so of pedaling through the lovely rain we came to a hairpin turn in the river, and the soothing white noise of rain drops on the water was interrupted by a sickening *conk* and the subsequent sound of my homemade weed guard grinding through gravel as the current forced the boat farther into the shallows.

I could not raise my prop up through the well to rescue it because its blades were not at the twelve-and-six position, and I could not lower it to get it to the twelve-and-six position because we were too shallow. All I could do is wait for us either to drift into deeper water or for some part to snap off. It felt like five minutes, though it was probably only twenty seconds. At last, we did drift into deeper water, and when Wade raised his drive, his prop was completely gone. Just gone. The shear pin had done its job and broken off, shedding the twenty-nine-dollar prop before allowing damage to the two hundred-dollar gears.

The river was narrow, and we got to the bank quickly. From the back seat, I talked him through how to install the spare prop we were carrying in the hold. He screwed it all together and tightened it down with the appropriate Allen wrench, which had already seen more action than I ever imagined it would.

"Dude . . ." he started, then paused, "something's not . . . sorry man, something's not quite right. I feel like I'm buzzing or something."

I knew the feeling well, and got right to the point. "Whadya have for breakfast?"

A granola bar was the answer.

"Yeah, those are mostly carbs and sugar," I said. "You need protein." This was knowledge I possessed not from college biology, in which I received a grade of D, but rather from life-long experience and trial and error managing my own sensitive blood sugar. I thankfully had never veered into full-blown diabetes, but I was sensitive enough that if I ever ate a sweet roll or a bowl of sugary cereal in the morning and forgot to have any significant protein, I could count on an eleven a.m. blood-sugar crash accompanied by a dull headache that led inevitably to vomiting. A couple of dozen episodes of that—and the realization of the pattern—was all it took to convince me to pay attention to protein in the morning. To avoid a splitting headache, each and every morning I had a date with the Ein sisters, Prot and Caff.

Wade was in great shape, unlike me, and was a seasoned runner despite a smoking habit that he already had when we met in high school and had tried many times to quit. But he was not in the habit of morning workouts and only ran in the evenings after work. He tore into a package of turkey jerky and within a few minutes was feeling better.

As we started out again, Wade with a new prop and a new blood-sugar level, I now noticed a clanging from my prop. If I pedaled slowly, it was silent, but if I pedaled with any real force, here came the rapid clanging, like the San Francisco street trolley on a Rice-a-Roni commercial. Since our nearly trip-ending Creaky and Squeaky episode, we were now loath to go any distance without addressing a strange noise. Wade paddled steadily on as I raised my prop, bent the L-shaped weed guard bracket one way, then lowered the drive and tried again. At first I would note an improvement, but again, pedal with any force and clang clang clang went the trolley. I repeated the whole process, bending the bracket another way, with the same effect. Finally, we realized that the homemade weed guard was not the problem. Rather, the ground-out had bent the prop's axle so that any extra force pushed the bracket into the crooked prop. The only way to prevent the clanging was to pedal easy—steady and easy.

It would not be the last time we grounded out that day—oh no. I had thought we would be well south and east of the limestone geology that created rocky-bottomed rivers up in the Balcones Escarpment of the Hill Country, but Texas was not quite so paint-by-numbers as that. We agreed Wade should keep his drive up for now and that we should treat it like a spare, at least until we got to obviously deeper water. After several more conks, scrapes, and scares, I began preemptively pulling my drive up each time Wade, sitting in front, noticed a change in the water's surface ahead of us—a rippling or a boiling.

Meanwhile, we both adopted the habit of regularly plunging our paddles vertically into the river to check its depth. His double-bladed paddle stayed locked together. I had found it useless to try to hold it or anything else in my right hand, and so I kept my paddle in two halves. I found that when I put the paddle end in the water, it twisted so violently against the current that I nearly lost my grip on it. I solved that problem by holding the paddle blade and instead, plunging the pole end, which put up almost no resistance, into the water.

We fell into a rhythm: shallow water ahead, "Prop coming up, dude. It's all you," I would announce. As the one who could hold a paddle, Wade shouldered the burden of keeping our boat facing downriver. The one thing I could do pretty effectively was "drag left." When the rudder wasn't cutting the mustard and we needed to make a tighter turn, I would drag my paddle in the river with my left hand and effect a much sharper left turn. This I did many times, and it made me feel like I was contributing more. In a minute or two, if we saw no more obvious surface signs of shallows, I would thrust my paddle down like a Viking draftsman checking the depth of the Thames or the Seine whilst pillaging monasteries, and if I didn't hit the bottom, I would announce, "Droppin' prop!" This routine was so constant on day three that I ceased using the drive well's plastic cover at all, and just shoved it under my seat to get it out of the way. If a little water came through the well, it certainly wasn't any more than had come over the gunwale on the lake the day before.

I began to deduce a useful above-water clue to where the river was deepest. Almost always, the riverbank was steeper on one side than the other. While one bank would gradually rise out of the water with a beach-like gentleness, with weeds emerging before the gravel showed itself, the opposite bank might be lined with boulders offering no easy place to land, or else the bank would rear up steeply at a forty-five-degree angle or even a sheer bluff face. It now seems too obvious to write, but eventually we figured out that the geology below the waterline was most likely the same as it was above: the steeper the bank, the deeper the river on that side, and so we began defaulting to whichever side of the river had the steeper bank.

~~~~~

Shallower water created swifter water, and while these were by no means Class V rapids, or really even Class I, they were sufficiently exciting for a guy with a stroke and a novice paddler. I gave Wade all the moral support I could and described how Kirstin's brother, Greg, a professional river guide in Colorado, had called out to us from the back of his raft during my prestroke life: "One hard on the left . . . Two hard on the right." A few times, I gave similar instructions in an attempt to help keep our heading through this swift section.

At one point, we came upon a large snag in the river, more like a stump protruding out of the water. We were moving relatively quickly and there was no way to avoid it. When we hit the snag, the strong current forced the upriver side of the boat down, and Wade leaned to the low side to dig with his paddle.

"High side!" I shouted, "Lean to the high side!"

SIXTEEN

THE RIGHTS OF MAN

"Whatever is my right as a man is also the right of another; and it becomes my duty to guarantee as well as to possess."

—THOMAS PAINE,
RIGHTS OF MAN, 1791

"HIGH SIDE!" We both leaned to the right, the high side, and soon the kayak leveled itself and spun off the stump. Our adrenaline was up, as we had come a hair's breadth from a complete dump, but we were okay and facing downriver once again.

Soon, we looked up atop the steep right bank and spied a pair of wild turkeys roosting on a rail fence, so still we thought they might have been decoys or 3D archery targets until one turned its head. With the best vision of any game animal in Texas, they watched us warily as we floated past.

An hour later we were in another winding section when we rounded a hairpin to find the entire Nueces River blocked by a fallen willow. Fortunately, the river was lazy at this point, even though it was narrow, and so we could take our time and talk through the conundrum. We might have tried powering through some thinner branches on the left side, but it looked like too much of a squeeze. So we first tried river-right but couldn't get through. We backed up, me pedaling backward, Wade paddling backward, and studied the middle section. If we could break enough branches off in the middle section, we might be able to pull the boat over with the props up. Broadside to the tree and facing the right bank, Wade and I started snapping and cracking branches. Two minutes later we were over the tree, but with a hundred sticks and a thousand slender willow leaves in the cockpits. It was as if the *Compton Comet*, not satisfied with its camo pattern, had donned a ghillie suit.

The last close call for the day was another rapid section in which Wade had to weave us through an obstacle course of snags. The front of the boat cleared one especially angry, crooked snag that turned horizontally toward the boat, but the current caught the front of the boat and turned it too soon, like an eighteen-wheeler jumping a curb. His seat had cleared the snag but my seat had not. Thankfully, it was on my left, so I was able to grab the angry branch with Lefty and push on it to avoid being impaled and dragged out of the boat.

It had been a long, slow day, with no landmarks to help us gauge our speed and progress, until at last, houses on the left signaled we had now kayaked fifty miles. Had we quit right then, it would have been significantly farther than I had ever traveled on a river before under human power.

Reaching the Highway 666 bridge, the Bridge of the Beast, meant we had made it 54.6 miles. It was late afternoon and time to find a spot to camp. Islands were fair game, and there were a considerable number of those upriver, which we had exploited on our first night at the head of the lake. But I knew there would not be enough to rely on those solely. Nor was I naive enough to believe that late every afternoon we would encounter a kindly landowner who would invite us to camp on his property, as had happened the previous night.

Rather, at some point I knew we would have to fall back on our rights, which I found on the Texas Parks and Wildlife website in a long and convoluted document citing snippets of case law here and there for well over a century. On a page titled Lawful Activities Along Navigable Streams, I had found that, "Texas courts have recognized that a member of the public may engage in a variety of lawful activities along a navigable stream. Besides boating, persons may swim, float, walk, wade, picnic, camp, and (with a license) fish. Public use must be confined to the stream bed and, to a limited extent, the banks."

Elsewhere on the site I found:

> On a navigable stream, the public has the right to use the streambed and the banks of the river only up to the point where public ownership ends and private ownership begins. This is known as the gradient boundary line, which is defined as the line located midway between the lower level of the flowing water after that just reaches the cut bank and the higher level just to the top of the bank. This definition is complicated and the line will differ for each property.

Of course, having rights does not mean that anyone else will understand them, let alone respect them when they are invoked. So we had resolved ahead of time that if we were ever confronted by a property owner, we would start by killing them with kindness, asking permission or forgiveness even if there was nothing to be forgiven for. We would assure them that we would leave no trace, that we would build no fire, make no loud noises, and would be gone at sunrise, all of which would have been true, as that was our decided modus operandi. If all of that failed, we would appeal to a higher power and offer them fifty dollars in cash. And if even that failed, we would move along and try another bank a few minutes farther downriver.

About forty-five minutes beyond the bridge, at around mile fifty-six, I spied a textbook river-camping site: a sandy beach jutting out a little into the river, with a long, high bank leading up to a clearing. Lifting the props and beaching the boat, I screwed one of my bright orange

Textbook river-camping site for night three.

stakes into the sand and tied the boat to it with a thick red rope. Then we dumped out the drybag, and Wade pitched the tent well below the gradient boundary line of the streambed. In fact, we were able to pitch our tent ten feet from the water's edge but no more than about four inches above the water's surface. Both textbook and beautiful.

We had taken our double-bladed paddles apart and stowed each half in the rod holders on either side of the seats, so we hung our blue long-sleeve shirts on the paddles, looking like baby-blue ramparts on a royal barge, to try and get them to dry. Dinner was another round of high-tech Omeals: chicken creole for Wade, lentils with beef for me.

That night, we left the rainfly off to ventilate the tent more. So naturally, at midnight, the skies opened up, and Wade had to scramble in the dark and the rain to get the fly on and rotate it to its correct position.

But I fell back to sleep with a smile on my face, a deep satisfaction that we were doing what we had set out to do: we were camping down a river to the sea.

SEVENTEEN

PALMETTOS AND PACHANGAS

"Be not forgetful to entertain strangers: for thereby some have entertained angels unawares." —HEBREWS 13:2

AS THE BLACK OF THE TENT'S INTERIOR lightened to the gray of morning, we ground into our slow-motion routine to get back on the water. Grunting and struggling to sit up, I rolled off my sleeping mat, which resembled an inflatable pool lounge, pulled its plug, then began the long process of snapping the edges together and then, with my left hand, rolling it up as tightly as I could and working it back and forth to get it into its stuff sack.

For bedding, Wade and I had each brought a twin-size flat sheet that we packed into ziplock bags each morning before they went into the duffle. At these temperatures, the sheet was just right.

The slowness of my morning routine was exacerbated by a new wrinkle—I took a bath in the river. Taking my shirt off but leaving my pants on, I waded in and carefully sat down in eight inches of water amid a sparse field of water plants. The temperature was perfect. I clutched the small bottle of Wilderness Wash with my claw-like right hand and managed to pour a few dollops of the soap into my left. I had bought this all-purpose soap—which cleans dishes, hair, body and clothes without polluting the water—years earlier, but it had sat unused under my

Day Four

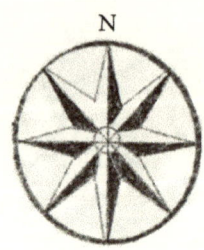

Mute Swan
Cygnus olor

Dwarf Palmetto
Sabal minor

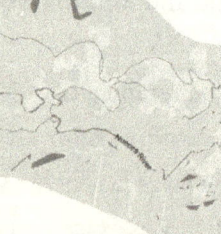

Robstown

Calallen Dam

Hazel Bazemore
County Park

bathroom sink, a wilderness bath never quite seeming worth the hassle until today, my fourth day since a shower.

As Wade was collecting his things, he found a huge cow patty just outside the tent that had not been there the previous evening. Apparently, we had a very large visitor in the night of which neither of us heard—likely a testament to robust snoring—or smelled, an equally impressive testament to how "nose blind" we had become in our own pungent company. "Think about that," Wade said earnestly. "A cow came and took a gigantic crap two feet away from us, and we smell so bad it didn't faze us." The cow must have visited after the rain and left its housewarming gift then, else Wade would have stepped right in it and probably have gone down hard in his scramble to get the rain-fly on the tent.

"Holy shit!" Wade exclaimed. I thought perhaps he was commenting on the pile of excreta, but then I followed his gaze upriver about fifty yards and soon saw the object of his shock. There, a large swan glided motionless along the still river, with three little cygnets floating on all sides of her like rowboats escorting a tall ship across a harbor. They were mute swans, with pure white bodies, black masks, and orange bills.

The sight made a deep impression on both of us, something so familiar in a city park but so completely unexpected on this wild stretch of river. Were we really seeing this? Ducks? No. Geese? No. Definitely swans. I later learned that mute swans are invasive exotics, brought from Central Asia during the 1800s, when the apparent goal of every American aristocrat was to own as many exotic species of plant and animal as possible. When the swans inevitably escaped their confines, like hogs, feral breeding populations spread across the continent, and woe to whichever native species would have to share their ecological niche. Invasive or not, there was magic in this still, early morning moment. This was not just any day, nor would it become one.

THE RIVER NUTS

As the tent and rain fly were still wet, I suggested Wade take the tent up the hill and set it in the direct sun while we ate and got dressed. I sat on the edge of the *Comet* and ate a tortilla smeared with peanut butter. Wade and I worked together to pump water out of the river through my little filter, and we added cold brew concentrate to it and drank it straight out of my old, banged-up aluminum pitcher.

This might have seemed like an extraordinary measure to get our morning coffee. But, as coffee drinkers know, coffee and the caffeine it carries are as strong an addiction as any in the human condition. Once on a camping trip when there were no other alternatives, I dry-swallowed a packet of instant coffee—true story. I often recalled the account of Stephen F. Austin, who, on his way from the Austin Colony to Mexico City, was faced with a choice between going without caffeine one day or building a fire to make coffee and therefore risking giving away his position to hostile Comanches in the area. The father of Texas opted to risk his life for his caffeine fix, and barely escaped. We were as serious about avoiding the caffeine withdrawal headache, but we had made a decision not to bring a stove or to worry about heating water, first because it was summer and we did not think hot beverages would appeal, and second, a stove, even a hiking stove, takes up space and adds weight.

It was almost nine before we finally got on the river, but within thirty minutes we were pulling over because Wade was again not feeling right. As on the previous morning, I asked him what he had for breakfast. There was a long silence before he answered . . . "A Pop Tart."

"Dude—protein," was all I said.

"Yeah, I know. I was so busy back there trying to get ready I just forgot."

It was true. Pitching camp and breaking camp were hard on him. I was pulling as much of my own weight as possible, but the lion's share of bending over and lifting and rolling and stuffing and hoisting the drybag into position and strapping everything down and pushing the boat in still fell to him. It was odd that for both of us, it was not the traveling that was strenuous; it was when we stopped to camp that the real exertion began.

He broke out the same bag of jerky he had the previous morning, and within ten minutes he again had stabilized, and we were back on the river.

We now entered a distinctly lazy, still stretch of river we instantly named "the bayou section." If you were a filmmaker in South Texas and wanted to fake a scene in Louisiana, this would have been perfect. There were even a few towering baldcypresses growing at the water's edge, a sight we hadn't seen since Austin.

The thin, twisting shape of the river meant lots of "sweepers," trees that overhung the river and were so named for their tendency to sweep any loose items out of boats—hats, paddles, even people if the conditions were right. Because of the meandering nature of the river and our natural desire to take the shortest possible route, we were constantly aiming for the inside lane of the grand prix race track, so we were constantly under or almost under sweepers. This put us right into cobwebs, which in turn brought us face to face with large brown spiders, known affectionately as—and I am not making this up—"rabid wolf spiders." Many of these arachnids apparently were discontented with this area and desired transport downriver and so began dropping into the boat like hobos jumping onto passing trains. Every ten minutes, when we realized another one had stealthily dropped onto the brim of one of our boonie hats, we cussed and thrashed and ripped off our hats and shook them to fling the spiders into the river. I was grateful anew for the sun gaiter that covered my ears, nose, and mouth.

Now, for the second time on the trip, we saw something dark in our peripheral vision drop and splash into the water. We were confused because it wasn't a fish blowup; you can tell the difference in sound between something that jumps out of the water and then lands in it again and something that simply falls into the water. Judging from the splash it had to have been as heavy as a turtle, but it could not have been a turtle because the tree branches, always willow, were spindly and nothing a turtle could climb.

Finally, we understood what we were seeing: dark brown snakes were falling out of the trees into the river. And now we had something besides rabid wolf spiders to watch for in the branches above us. We never got a clean look at one, but based on size, coloration, and habitat, subsequent research told me they were either cottonmouths, southern water snakes, green water snakes, or plain-bellied water snakes.

There was no current in this wide section, known to river travelers as a "pool." But forty yards ahead, a log drifted quickly right to left, then disappeared. I had just seen the apex predator of the Nueces. Not the alligator gar—I had just seen an alligator. We were in the bayou section, indeed.

Late that morning, we passed beneath a wooden footbridge suspended over the river by a couple of rusty cables. It was amazing that a three-foot-wide bridge could be seen from space with the right equipment, but I had found it on Google Maps' satellite layer a week earlier and added it to my river notes, and so we knew we were at mile 62.75.

I also knew from that landmark that we likely were within twenty minutes of something we found on the map called "New Camp Spot." The Google Map had a bed icon there, as if it might have been a bed and breakfast, but the image did not show a structure or even a road into the area. When one clicked on the pin, a single comment appeared, which simply said, "What is this place?"

When we reached a bend in the river, we saw it, the name summed it all up—it was a camp spot, apparently a new one, and that was it. A couple of logs had been cut for benches, and there was a fire pit and a footpath coming from who-knows-where. We beached the boat. I disembarked on the river side as it was downhill, and it was much easier for me to get out of the boat downhill than uphill.

I then did something for the second time that day. I sat in the river, not as a bath this time but just as a soak. As I sat there soaking, I studied the far bank. It was starting to look more like South Texas. The thorny huisatch, blooming with its poofy yellow flowers, had begun farther upstream. Huisache is a kind of acacia tree, which according to the Bible was specified by God as the material the Hebrews should use to build the Ark of the Covenant. I supposed this was a holy land in its own right, if you knew where to look.

I glimpsed the occasional mesquite, as well. To my surprise, though, mesquite never pervaded the river banks or even made much of an appearance at all despite its utter domination of every other landscape in this region. Willow continued as the dominant tree until the final miles. There was also plenty of water hyacinth, a fast-growing invasive from South America. It is problematic in the way that all invasives are problematic, but it does have a lovely purple flower.

After a lunch of cold barbecue chicken squeezed from a plastic envelope onto tortillas, we got back on the river and headed into another series of hairpin turns where the river was so narrow I almost could have touched both banks with outstretched arms, if only both arms worked. We squeezed between sweepers left and sweepers right that almost touched in the middle of the river to form a tunnel. A rescue plane would have no chance of spotting us here.

~~~~~

At mile sixty four, we began to see houses on our right. This signaled Robstown, but I suspected it was not an entry into the city that would have made its founders swell with civic pride. We were basically passing a series of scary water-front junkyards, replete with vicious dogs and sketchy piers that were collapsing into the water in super slow motion. The alligator I had seen earlier, who was clearly content to live and let live at the distance we saw him or her, was not unsettling to me; I actually thought it was pretty neat. These dogs were much scarier, and I had no doubt that if there had not been a chain-link fence holding them back, they would have swum out to us, boarded the kayak, and torn us both limb from limb.

In time, as we passed into Corpus Christi proper, the houses got intermittently nicer, with huge mowed yards and landscaping, then would backslide into an architectural style known as meth-lab revival.

To our left, the vegetation marked another transition in the river, as willows slowly began to be replaced by dwarf palmettos. At this, the river deepened and began a long straightaway directly to the east. The lack of obstacles in the river, such as sweepers and shallows, led to conversations about other things entirely.

"This is sort of a random question," I said, "but where are your parents buried?"

"My dad's buried in a veteran's cemetery in Killeen that opened right around the time he died," Wade said. His dad had served during the Korean War before going to work for ARCO as an oil and gas operations manager in the Rio Grande Valley.

"But he was living in the Valley when he died, right?" I asked. Though memories were hazy, I was pretty sure I had attended his funeral in McAllen.

"Yeah, but he was never a fan of the Valley."

"Why's that?" I pried.

"I don't know, he just never really liked it there. He grew up in Freer. He didn't like it there either."

In that regard, Mr. Walker would have been the opposite of my dad, who loved South Texas so much he wrote ballets and orchestral suites about it, and when they wheeled his coffin out of First Presbyterian in McAllen, at his request, they played "For We Love Our Valley Home," a sort of rousing chamber-of-commerce march composed in the 1940s, blasting on the largest pipe organ south of San Antonio, a sixteen-piece orchestra, and a choir with the congregation standing and singing the lyrics printed in the bulletin:

> For we love our Valley home way down upon the Rio Grande
> Land of yours and land of mine, land of palm trees and the
>   bright sunshine
> There we'll live in paradise for roses bloom on every hand
> For we love our Valley home down upon the Rio Grande!

But I suppose it made sense that you would want to like the place where your bones would spend the next few centuries. And I did hope Mr. Walker liked Killeen.

~~~~~

At last we began to see covered picnic tables on our right, a sign that we had reached mile seventy and Hazel Bazemore County Park. We continued cranking past the tables for fifteen minutes until reaching a concrete boat ramp at the park's east end. There, we raised the props, disembarked, and Wade dragged the 'yak most of the way out of the water. This marked the first time in two days we had access to a trash can, and Wade extracted the ziplock bag from under his seat that now held empty Omeals bags, Tuna Creations, Chicken Creations, the empty turkey jerky bag, cigarette butts, empty cigarette cartons, peanut butter cracker wrappers, Pop Tart wrappers, empty 5-Hour Energy bottles, and cold brew coffee shots.

I stood next to the *Comet* and bore weight through my hip and leg. From the top corner of the ramp, I watched a man backing his boat trailer into the water with his teenage son in the boat. When the motor reached the water line, the young man fired it up and the motor began vomiting water out the back. Then, the father tapped his truck's accelerator and pulled the boat back up to the parking lot. They were not putting the boat in the river but merely using the freshwater to clean the corrosive saltwater out of the motor after a day of fishing. It was another sign that we were nearing the end of our journey. We were now within two miles of the dam that separated freshwater from brackish water.

Little did we know this then, but this unassuming county park had a distinction: in the fall, it is one of the hottest spots in North America for viewing the migration of raptors. Not only can a sharp-eyed birder identify osprey, red-tailed hawks, red-shouldered hawks, sharp-shinned hawks, Cooper's hawks, Harris's hawks, kestrels, and Mississippi kites, but on certain autumn days, one hundred thousand broad-winged hawks can be seen overhead, migrating south for the winter. Volunteers with high-powered binoculars and clickers will stand on a deck at the park's east edge and mumble to one another, "Mississippi kite... two," or "There's a new kettle forming... broad-wings," a kettle being the upward spiral of raptors riding thermal updrafts to gain altitude before gliding to the next updraft to form a new kettle. (They are called kettles due to their resemblance to steam rising from a kettle of boiling water.)

But it wasn't fall, and instead of being overrun with birders, the park was nearly empty on this Tuesday, with only a few families fishing from the bank.

After a twenty-minute stretch and smoke break, we launched again and soon a sign warned of a dam in six thousand feet. Wade said he thought a mile was 5,714 feet, but he wasn't positive if that was a mile or Nolan Ryan's career strikeouts, because he was always confusing the two. (For the record, a mile is 5,280 feet.) Either way, we were now roughly a mile from said dam, and I told Wade that the way I usually thought of a mile was as just more than seventeen football fields.

PALMETTOS AND PACHANGAS

About thirty minutes later, we began seeing figures who looked to be standing ankle deep in the middle of the river. "Either one of those guys is Jesus or that's the dam," said Wade. Although we had scouted Calallen Dam the previous week, we did not know just what the dam would look like today, so I steered us hard river-right, and we tentatively crept up to it along the bank. Immediately, we began receiving helpful but forceful advice from the anglers who had appeared to walk on water: "Go over here, over here. Get out over here and we'll carry it over. Pablo," one called out to another on shore, "ándale, pues, help us carry it over there, ese! Over there, over there!" We could not get a word in edgewise. It was clear they owned this section of the river, and we should just go with the flow, do exactly as suggested, and be grateful.

As we looked up to the bank, we saw a group of about ten people clustered around a grill. Empty Michelob cans littering the ground betrayed a long afternoon of day-drinking. We climbed out of the boat, and Wade and two fishermen pulled the 'yak onto the gently sloping concrete spillway, where less than an inch of water was trickling over—not enough to move the hefty *Compton Comet*.

They offered us as many spicy beef sausage links wrapped in toasted tortillas as we wanted, and may I just say they were grilled to perfection. I made the acquaintance of Nick, who looked about sixty and was rail thin and weathered, with bushy white hair and a gray moustache, faded blue jeans, and a plain white T-shirt. Nick was born in Guanajuato, in central Mexico, but had lived in Corpus forty-five years. He and his buddies, many of whom were house painters, came here to the dam multiple times a week to fish for gar. They even built their own permanent benches at the spot, an endearing bit of extra-jurisdictional initiative. I asked if they ate the gar, as I had heard they were not good. But Nick and company gave the meat an enthusiastic thumbs-up, when breaded and fried. Then Nick's young friend showed me a picture on his cell phone, one I suspect he referenced often, of him standing next to a six-foot gar hanging from a tree.

I sat on a wooden railing and ate my sausage wraps and guzzled the bottled water handed to me. We spoke of fishing, the river, the weather, hometowns, my stroke, and Wade and I endured a tipsy, spirited argument between two of them over whether more members of the Dallas Cowboys or the Pittsburg Steelers were gay. I took from context that the football team with fewer homosexual players would be the better team, but I didn't pursue the subject. We were not in Austin anymore, that was for sure. In Austin, as in much of the Western world, we largely had moved beyond discussions of sexual orientation and were now on to the question of gender itself. I recently had been required to fill out a health-care form for my job at the university, and when I got to "gender," I was given seven options from which to choose. The point being, we definitely were not in Austin.

After about forty-five minutes, my internal timer went off, and I deemed it time to get back on the river. They gave us water, Sam's Cola, and Orangette for the remainder of the journey.

Five of them carried the boat over the spillway and floated it amidst jagged rubble that protruded above the water on the dam's downstream side. Before I even knew what was happening, two men had grabbed me under each arm and were virtually carrying me over super sketchy concrete blocks toward the boat, while I attempted to explain what I might be capable of or what looked too dangerous. "Hey . . . okay, well, yeah . . . thank you. Woah, this uh—this hey, okay. So right here, woah, okay, yeah," all the while just being carried along as if by a river of humanity. They were going to get this disabled gringo back in his boat by hook or by crook, even if they disabled him more in the process, and perhaps themselves.

Wade was still talking to the Steelers fan, Jesse, back by the grill, so I yelled back, *"Dude! The train is leaving the station!"* I later learned that at this moment our host was trying to extend his generosity by getting

With new friend Nick.

Wade to accept a few bottles of Michelob and, when Wade declined those, then a palmful of marijuana buds. Wade tried to decline them too, but Jesse wouldn't hear of it. (I wouldn't know any of this until days later, when Wade texted me a picture of the buds and, after I had asked why he was texting me a photo of broccoli, got an explanation of what it actually was and how he had come by it.)

Wade gave his parting thanks and fast-walked toward the kayak. Then I plopped hard into my seat, rocking the boat violently, and Wade plopped into his. "Thank you!" we both cried out, "'preciate it! God bless!"

Fishermen carry the Compton Comet over the crude dam marking the beginning of the Calallen Reservoir.

We were full of warm, delicious sausage and tortillas, fully hydrated, and felt like we had made some genuine connections during the hour-long layover. Our faith in humanity had been bolstered by the hospitality when we marooned ourselves on the lake, then dinged by the flinty old couple that denied us simple access to the river behind their tackle store, then restored by the offer of the camp just after that. Now with this portage-and-meal combo, our faith in humanity was soaring off the charts.

EIGHTEEN

BRACKISH

THERE WAS SOMETHING ABOUT THE EPISODE at Calallen Dam that combined several themes I had been thinking about. One was the historical echo of light-skinned visitors arriving by boat in a land long occupied by dark-skinned locals. Though their surnames were European—Spanish—I have no doubt that genetically, these were largely the same folks that Cabeza de Vaca first encountered just up the coast almost five centuries earlier. And while his time among the indigenous people of North America got off to a rough start—being enslaved and abused—by the end of his ten-year journey across the continent, he was being carried before a throng of Indians, hailed as a healer, a holy man, and a hero. I too had been carried before a throng of brown-skinned natives, though not so much as a healer as someone who needed healing.

No doubt, Wade and I were visitors passing through a land that they thoroughly "owned." We were the invasive exotics, but there was a sense in which our two varietals—pink-skinned and brown-skinned—had managed to find an equilibrium and coexist. While European invasive exotics of an earlier time were not so satisfied to live and let live, we seem to have found a steady state and were on pace to become one people, hybridizing more with every generation—not so different from the barred owls and spotted owls in the Pacific Northwest.

Whites were invasive exotics in Texas. But so were the Indians, inasmuch as all *Homo sapiens* were invasive exotics in the New World.

Indeed, we are all invasive exotics in Asia, and Australia, and Europe. Yes, humans were once invasive exotics on every continent in the world except Africa.

I'm not saying that alarms about invasive exotics among wildlife are not worthy of our attention and efforts to control, be they zebra mussels, Asian carp, or giant salvinia. I am saying that to some extent, invasive exotics are an inevitable part of the web of life. And however ecologically impure they may be, without a doubt our trip would have been less interesting without the purple water hyacinths from South America, or the mute swans from Central Asia, or the Homo sapiens originally from Africa, who got here by way of Siberia and who were grilling domesticated hogs first introduced from Europe.

Now we were in the Calallen Reservoir section of the Nueces. The brackish water had begun, and immediately we began seeing silvery mullet, a saltwater fish, leaping out of the water over and over. I refilled my bottle again with river water, unsure of whether or not the LifeStraw would still do the trick. When I tasted it, I could detect no salt. It might have been salty enough for the mullet way up here by the dam, but it was not too salty for the LifeStraw.

Now, on our left, was a massive city park named for two native sons of Corpus Christi, Terry and Bobby Labonte, who Wade informed me were famous NASCAR drivers. Appropriately named, I suppose, as the roar of the interstate highway permeated every part of the park.

The sun was getting low, and we did not know where we were going to camp, as, of course, we never did. As we crossed under I-37 we aimed for a boat ramp on our right. "Do we just camp under the freeway?" Wade asked. Wade had been through a lot, and I decided that if he wanted to pitch camp under a roaring freeway, just to be off the water, I was good with it. It wasn't exactly getting away from it all, but it would have given us both a lot of insight into what living homeless was like and would probably yield a few memorable vignettes.

"It's entirely up to you," I said with a smile. "The executive decision is yours."

He walked a few feet from the boat ramp and just there, beside the trash-strewn asphalt, was a patch of worn dirt and grass where the tent could sit just so. He snapped a picture with his phone and brought it to me as I sat in the boat. "I don't even need to see it, dude. I trust you completely."

Just then a fisherman walked up, stood in the very spot Wade was considering for the tent, and started casting his line. "Well," said Wade, "I guess that answers that."

He got back in the boat and we started down the widening river, me trying to sell him on the idea that there were plenty of spots river-left that we could get into. Some might require a little more effort than others, but there were definitely little clearings here and there where the tent would fit.

At 73.4 miles, we crossed under a railroad bridge and a few minutes later spotted a relatively clear bank on the right, about seven feet up. We beached the boat, and I wedged my paddle into the mud to hold the kayak still as Wade scouted the top of the bank. We could hear a few barking dogs in a far-distant subdivision, but visually, we were completely isolated. It would do. We were not entirely within the law, as we were clearly up on top of the bank, above the gradient boundary line, but with the setting sun it became a matter of safety winning out over legality, and besides, it was not entirely clear that this land was not public. Nevertheless, we now were "stealth camping" so as to attract the least attention.

First, Wade had to get me up the seven-foot bank. This he did, at my request, by standing on top of the bank and holding one end of his long, double-bladed paddle. He extended the other end down to me, and when I had grasped it and had my feet reasonably well under me, he commenced pulling my 190 pounds up the bank, leaning backwards as if we were in a tug of war, one in which gravity was completely on my side. Getting me up the bank required the exact same posture and exertion he had to use when easing the *Compton Comet* down the steep ramp to the river below the lake.

With me up, Wade then pulled the boat up and into high grass so it wasn't visible from the water. Since our tent was green, it blended nicely with our environs, even if it wasn't camo.

I did the math in my head and texted Kirstin with my new estimate of when we would be done. Whereas I had originally thought it could be four o'clock the following afternoon, I now thought it could be as early as one.

When he had finished setting up the tent, Wade panted, "Dude... I love you, man, but I am *done*. I can't do this again. I'm physically exhausted."

His comment implied that he wasn't exactly sure where in the trip we were. Maybe it was delirium, or maybe it was that he had long ago ceded all the logistical decisions to me. But whichever the case, he wanted to make it crystal clear that if we had another night of camping before we made it to the bay, he was out. It was the recreational equivalent of "giving notice" at a job. "I know you're done," I said, "and I'm done too. This is it. This is our last night."

Night fell with a clear sky that invited stargazing, but soon mosquitoes forced us off our stools and into the tent, where we could only see the brightest stars through the mesh roof. Poor Wade was so hot, he actually tried to go to sleep on his knees and elbows so that no part of his body was touching any other part of his body. It almost worked too, until his arms fell asleep before he did.

"I'm afraid I've wrecked our friendship." I said without any exaggeration or irony.

"Hardly, dude."

NINETEEN

THE OLD MEN...

WE AWOKE IN THE DARK and began preparing for our final push, me grunting and straining to sit up in the tent to take my anti-seizure medication, Wade taking his high-blood-pressure pill. It was in these early morning moments that the fact we actually had become old men was in sharpest focus.

Of course, we had first met in high school, and so much of the time we were together, our conversational patter reverted to the language and rhythm of the early 1980s, dude this and dude that, and plenty of teenage boy vulgarity, like linguistic snap shots in an old photo album, at once colorful as a dialect and also evidence of a poverty of expression that we defaulted to in the judgment-free, history-rich comfort of each other's company. But these were the times we came face to face with the odd reality, the creaks and snaps, our bodies echoing the creaks and squeaks of the kayak pedal drives, the fatigue, the back braces, the scorekeeping of who had evacuated when, my occasional inability to go No. 1 when I needed to, and Wade's jealousy over my being able to go No. 2. We were old, me much older than him due to that bad day I had two-and-a-half years earlier.

By first light, we were keen to get on the water and get cranking. For one thing, we were somewhere we really should not have been according to the letter of the law. For another, it was a cruel blue sky, and it was getting hotter by the moment. And for a third, I knew that we had two long straightaways due east, and that was the most concerning of all.

Day Five

Blue Crab
Callinectes sapidus

THE OLD MEN...

Summer mornings were stock-still with no breeze to relieve the smothering humidity on the coast. But I knew that as the day wore on, the wind would grow steadily out of the Gulf and become relentless as we approached afternoon. Even having little freeboard—with only a few inches of hull showing above the water line—and sitting in a nearly fully reclined position that minimized wind resistance, with the wind we might be screwed if we dallied in camp too long. We had come too far and invested too much to come up just short of the goal. I had to see the ocean.

So we broke camp quickly, with only the essentials in our blood streams: caffeine and protein. No Pop Tarts, no bath in the river, no setting the tent out to dry. We were on a mission: pack up, leave no trace, and get cranking. Despite our hurry, I took pride in the fact we left not one scrap of trash, no matter how small. All we took with us were a few mosquitoes, and we doubted they'd be missed.

~~~

By seven-thirty we began passing houses on the right, which, according to the laminated index cards that rode in the pocket of my always-on black-and-yellow life jacket, marked mile seventy-four. The sun had only just risen and yet was nearly blinding as it reflected off the water. A row of tall, stately Washingtonia palms on our left were perfectly inverted in the glassy stillness of the river, a stillness only occasionally broken by a silvery mullet hopscotching its way across our path.

"About ten years ago," I said as we creaked along, "I got into the habit of trying to spot caracaras, you know, Mexican eagles, on the drive down to the Valley, either home or to South Padre. It was usually around this area, at least this latitude, that I would start to see 'em, sitting on a telephone pole or roosting in a dead tree. They're so distinctive, ya know, those white faces and crazy orange beaks.

"When my dad was near the end, I got the call—from my mom or from Erren, one—that hospice had come to the house, and he had gone

Washingtonia palms reflected in the still morning waters of the Nueces at Calallen.

on morphine. I emailed work and took off in my truck to McAllen to be at his side. I was passing the time driving by myself, looking and looking for caracaras, but hadn't spotted one yet. Then all the sudden, one came right over the road in front of me—just showed itself to me.

"When I reached McAllen, Dad was still alive, but he wasn't conscious. I've sort of always thought that his soul left him right about the time that caracara flew over my truck—that that was him telling me goodbye." My voice wavered.

"Wow," Wade said. "You could be right."

As we continued pedaling, I kept vacillating between the middle of the river—on the theory that the current was strongest there—and the east or left side of the river, which still tempted us with a sliver of shade from the few short trees that still tried to grow on the salty bank.

To our right just out of view was Pollywog Pond Bird and Wildlife Sanctuary, one of several projects at the Corpus end of the Nueces to preserve the river's natural beauty. This particular one was in view of both the golden arches of a McDonald's and the giant orange-striped W of a Whataburger, so close and yet so far. Miles to go before we'd eat.

We had also been noting for some time two parallel rows of evenly spaced white buoys, which I took for boating lanes of some kind. I wasn't sure which lane we were supposed to be in, but it didn't seem to matter.

We curved hard to the east and noted another change in the scenery, as trees of any height—palms, palmettos, even mesquites—suddenly vanished. A low-slung railroad bridge marked mile seventy-nine, our final unmistakable landmark.

TWENTY

. . . AND THE SEA

IT WAS LATE MORNING, and right on cue, the wind began picking up. I set a heading for the inside curve of another point that would require us to cross the widening river, and we cranked in silence against the wind.

Normally I would not be heartened to see the river enter an industrial section. Railroads running from the ship channel, mountains of quarried caliche and sand, power lines, gasworks, water stations, refineries, and highway bridges were not why I chose this river, or would choose any river. But they were welcome sights now, as I knew they heralded the goal.

After what seemed like an hour, we reached the point I had been aiming for, and we both were desperate to get out of the boat, our tailbones screaming for any change of position that might relieve the pressure for even five minutes. We spotted a muddy bank river-right where locals fished, raised the props, and beached the boat. No sooner were we grounded than—fully dressed in the long-sleeve shirt, gloves, boonie, long pants, AFO, Texas socks, and rubber sandals that had become as much a part of me as my own skin—I climbed out of the boat and eased down into the muddy shallows. I rolled onto my stomach, propping myself on my elbows to arch my spine concave in a position therapists call "prone on elbows" and yoga practitioners call "sphinx." The water was a perfect temperature, and I could have remained in sphinx for an hour without it seeming excessive.

. . . AND THE SEA

A bearded ruddy man sat in his pickup and asked if we had seen boaters on the water. As I was basically incapacitated by tailbone pain, Wade gamely began chatting him up between draws on his cigarette as I stared out at the water and listened.

The man ran a crabbing business, and the endless lines of white buoys we had been seeing for the past three hours were not boating markers but rather denoted blue-crab traps below. The man had five licenses for blue crabs, and each license allowed him two hundred traps. His workers would run up and down the brackish reservoir section of the river pulling up cage traps, emptying them into the boat, then rebaiting them with quartered chicken legs or cut-up hardhead catfish. He once sold them direct to the Landry's Seafood restaurant chain, but since the pandemic, he now just packed them on ice and sold them to a distributor down in Harlingen.

At the end of a thirty-minute break, I crawled back into the kayak, and we now headed into another long straightaway to the east. A steady breeze blew out of the Gulf, so steady that if we paused our pedaling for more than ten seconds, we slowed to a stop, then began inching backward up the river.

At a point where the adjacent highway nearly touched the river, we passed a park. We had reached mile eighty-two, and now had seen the spot where we would rendezvous with Kirstin. But we weren't finished yet. The mouth of the river and Nueces Bay lay two more miles ahead.

For the final hour, we pedaled on in near-complete silence. There was no chatter about high school days. No discussion of families or mutual friends. No historical asides or "little known facts." No amateur naturalist observations or calling attention to "pelican, ten o'clock." No reliving the perils of the trip or the blooper reel of the cow patty or the rabid wolf spiders or the raining of snakes. No more exclaiming *"ánda!"* or laughing about "What the shit?!" No more complaining about tailbones. Talking required energy, and here at the final hour and with the wind in our faces, every last bit of energy had to go through our feet and into our pedals. We had to make the goal. To somehow come up short now—to quit in mile twenty-five of the marathon—would be unbearable.

~~~

The river curved widely to the left, then back to the right, and at 12:32 p.m. on June 3, 2020, we landed on an oyster-strewn island that marked the mouth of the river and the head of Nueces Bay. We had done it—kayaked and camped eighty-four miles. We had done what I had dreamed of for so long, boated down a river to the sea. Check.

But there was no jumping up and down, no splashing about in the saltwater. (Wade scooped some up in his bottle and confirmed that the LifeStraw no longer worked; that was definitive proof that we had reached the sea.) There was only a calm smile from me, a cigarette for him, a deep breath, and a fist bump. I had planned for the past hour to repeat a version of what I had done during our last stop, to roll out of the boat and sit in the water on the sandy bottom, but here there was naught but razor-sharp oyster shells as far as I could have waded.

Laughing gulls with orange beaks and black heads covered the island, a nice welcoming committee again confirming that we indeed had reached the coast. To our right, in the distance, downtown Corpus Christi, "the body of Christ," a phrase I could never think of without following it with "broken for you." Growing up, each time we passed the bread during communion, we said, "This is the body of Christ, broken for you." Wade and I had probably exchanged this sacramental greeting during communion at a church camp during high school. Certainly now, we had broken our own bodies, if temporarily, for each other and for this experience.

We snapped a selfie with the bay in the background and texted it to Dave, the mutual friend through whom we had met each other all those decades ago, and who had worked so hard to help me find a

. . . AND THE SEA

"Made it." The goal reached: the Nueces Bay, and the selfie texted to Dave.

solution to keeping my foot on its pedal, and who had rescued the boat when it sank in Brushy Creek Lake with us in it. "Made it," was the only caption.

After fifteen minutes of savoring the accomplishment, we headed back upriver to meet Kirstin, cranking hard through the rough waves created by the turbulence of the river emptying into the choppy bay. With the wind now at our backs, we experimented with simply drifting, but of course this spun us around so that we weathervaned into the wind again and thus had no control over our direction. The drift took us quickly toward one bank, then another, until we resigned ourselves to the fact that we would never reach the extraction point unless we pedaled.

Now a yelp escaped my mouth as I cried out in pain. The tissue around my tailbone was so swollen and now stung so badly I thought my coccyx had finally broken through the skin. The pressure, the water, the heat, and the friction had pushed it to its limit. I figured I was fifteen minutes away from actual bleeding. The trip would not end a moment too soon. In short, Wade had busted his ass figuratively, and I had busted mine quite literally.

Just as the park came into view, I saw my white pickup pull in off the highway with Kirstin behind the wheel. I regard it still as one of my life's minor miracles; we could not have choreographed it more perfectly if we had been in continuous minute-by-minute contact. She was a beautiful sight on so many levels. I kissed her despite my five-day beard and what must have been a terrible, truly terrible stench.

As we offloaded the gear for the last time and strategized how to scoot the boat over the mud and rocks, then slide it along the grass, then under a steel cable that prevented cars from getting too close to the water, I said, "I don't give a rat's ass about this boat anymore. The only reason I'm putting it in the truck is because I'm committed to leave-no-trace."

An exhausted embrace at the truck marks the end of the journey.

Kirstin reinstalled my left-foot accelerator, I took the driver's seat, and we headed northwest along I-37 toward home, seeing the town names we had come to know, all in reverse—Calallen, Mathis, Swinney Switch. In San Patricio, we pulled over for gas. As the tank filled and Wade burned a cig near the entrance to the convenience store, I sat in the truck with Kirstin.

"I wonder what your next adventure will be," she said.

"I think I'm good for at least two years," I laughed, adjusting my tailbone, "maybe more."

"I wonder— I wonder if our ideas of what adventure is adjust over time to match our abilities," she offered.

"If that's the case, I think my next adventure may be birdwatching from a wheelchair," I said. Kirstin laughed as I gingerly climbed out of the truck and the pump clicked off. I think this exchange summed up the whole thing: adventure is entirely relative to ability.

When the pickup reached Three Rivers, we still had not eaten, and so I turned south, and in a few short miles we pulled into the Dairy Queen, which, as we all knew, was on the left. Since it is nearly impossible for me to eat while driving with one hand, we decided to go in, and I backed into a parking spot, the better to keep an eye on the loose contents of the pickup's bed and make sure they didn't walk off. The *Compton Comet* protruded across the sidewalk that ran alongside the building and nearly all the way to the restaurant's window. I tenderly extracted myself again from the driver's seat, and as I turned to inspect the position of the boat, I beheld a scene that summed up the whole trip perfectly: the fourteen-foot, gray camo, tandem pedal kayak, almost kissing the handicap parking sign.

The physical results of the trip were keenly felt at the time but short-lived. They consisted of a mild sunburn to my face and neck despite all my various forms of coverage, a rather impressive case of diaper rash that covered my buttocks and took a week to clear up, and swollen tissue

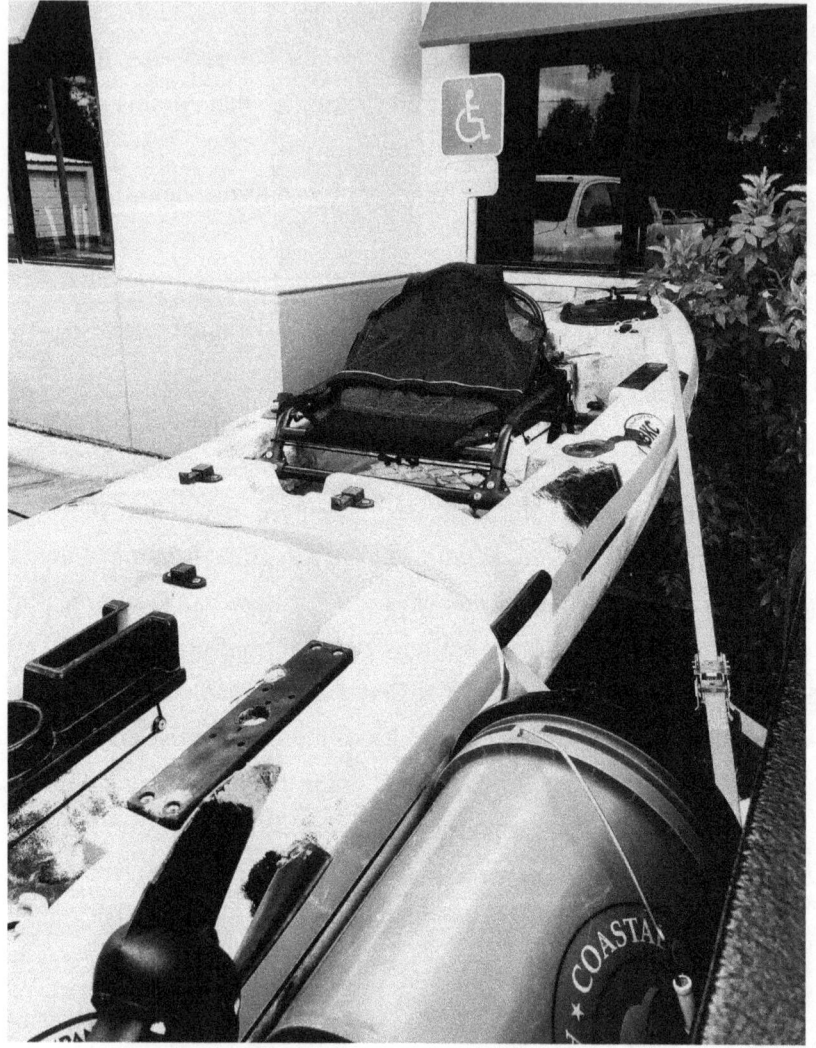
"Adventure is entirely relative to ability."

around my tailbone that took two weeks to resolve completely. Wade's after-action report consisted mainly of digestive issues for some ten days. "It felt like my body simply couldn't digest any solid food I put into it," he told me.

The psychological effects of the trip on me were two in number, and probably would last a lifetime. And they were really two sides of

the same coin. The heads side of the coin was confidence. I now knew that if I really wanted to do something, and was patient enough and inventive enough and had at least one really good friend, I could probably pull it off.

The tails side of that coin was an inconvenient loss of excuses. I could not as easily "play the stroke card" in situations I might have previously. When I felt puny and did not think I could navigate some unmowed area or uneven ground, I would think back to the time I dragged myself out of the lake and onto a weedy bank when Dave and I had swamped. When I wished I could avoid mowing the yard with one arm, I would then think about the times I wrestled the entire hundred-pound boat across the driveway and lifted it onto steel cots. And when I would rather not get wet, I would remember how gleefully and willingly I had rolled my whole body into a muddy river, right next to a sign that read, "CAUTION – SNAKES AND ALLIGATORS," just to cool off.

THE RIVER NUTS

When we got home, I tried to sum up the trip for friends with four lists:

Things seen: alligator gar in the hundreds, snakes falling out of trees into the water, huge barred owls crossing the river in front of us, green herons in the dozens, violent storms, peaceful rain, tear-jerking sunrises and sunsets, a family of swans gliding on the water, an alligator, a severed hog's leg, Spanish moss, fishermen under bridges, bald-cypresses, palmettos, wild turkeys, willows in the millions, rabid wolf spiders.

Things heard: barred owls, great horned owls, bullfrogs, coyotes, crickets, barking dogs, lonely trains, songbirds, and laughing gulls.

Things tasted: tuna, peanut butter, cold coffee, and tortillas.

Things smelled: ourselves.

~~~~~

Three weeks after our trip down the Nueces, our neighbors' hackberry tree lost a gigantic limb. This led to two days of tree work as men with chainsaws and climbing gear took down that tree and two similar ones that were threatening their house. We had two dead oaks in our own yard that had long been candidates for removal, so I invited the foreman of the crew to come over and give us a quote.

I struggled the gate open to let him into the backyard and began leading him past the ramshackle boat port under which sat the kayak. The foreman's eyes grew wide. "Wow," he said, "is that a kayak?"

"Yeah—yeah it is, a two-man, a tandem."

It was clear he wasn't an expert, as he momentarily thought that the back was the front, but I could see some intense interest in his eyes.

"It looks really stable," he said. "Almost like you could stand up in it."

"Yeah, it's pretty neat—a pedal kayak."

Finally, I was able to get him away from the boat and continued leading him back into the yard to show him the dead trees. He figured it would be about a half day's work for the crew and gave me the estimate: six hundred twenty dollars.

On the way back out of the gate, he loitered again next to the boat. "Wow," he said again, "that is really something."

"Yeah," I said. "A friend and I just went eighty-six miles in it, George West to Corpus Christi. Camped the whole way. Pretty wild."

"Is that right?!" he said. "What is that river? I'm not even sure what that would be."

"It's the Nueces," I said. "It was quite an adventure."

"I bet it was. That's a nice boat!"

This guy wants my boat, I thought. I bet he would pay me five hundred dollars plus trade the tree work for it. I looked at the boat, then looked at him, then back at the boat.

I decided against it.

AFTERWORD

BY WADE WALKER

AS I WRITE THIS, please know a few things: 1) I've not read a word of the story you just enjoyed; 2) I'm not even sure this will make the cut for the book; 3) I lived it.

I've known Avrel since 1984 and can say that since that time, he's brought enrichment and many wonderful memories into my life. I consider him a great friend, a confidant, a hero, and a great human. Throughout this story, however, if he was completely honest and open about the social dynamics of this adventure, you may question this statement. I'll explain.

Our earlier years together consisted of a very typical eighties upbringing. Ave and I met through mutual friends. Our initial interactions consisted of parties, beer, music, a church camp, parties, and beer—wash, rinse, repeat. We grew up in far South Texas away from the rest of the world, or so it felt. Looking back on it, the friendships and freedoms we were able to experience will endure in our memories and in the stories we share for years to come. It was an incredible upbringing.

In the winter of 1984, I met up with four guys—Avrel, David McLeod, David's brother John, and Steve Rodriguez—as a prelude for one of our party weekends. Avrel, Dave, John, and Steve were jamming at Steve's and, lo and behold, their drummer had skipped practice. Well, I'm itching to get to the party, so to move this process along, I picked up a pair of sticks and started trying to pick up a beat. The next thing I know, I'm buying a drum set and we're setting up shop in the game room of my

AFTERWORD

parent's house. From there, we played a few parties and performed at a school concert until we graduated from high school in 1985.

As we all went our separate ways to college and beyond, we kept in touch. In the early nineties, I moved to Austin. Shortly thereafter, Avrel moved to Austin and shortly after that, so did Dave. As the years ensued, we all married, had children, and were busy building our lives. Oddly enough, we lived in the same neighborhood, and from time to time, we'd end up just knocking on each other's door if we found ourselves near each other's house. And, of course, the Annual Seale Christmas Party was a great time to catch up with Ave, Kirstin, and the boys.

Despite all I've mentioned, my best memories with Avrel were our monthly lunches at Burger-Tex on the Drag in Austin. Aside from the best burgers I've ever had, it allowed us to have some very interesting and personal conversations. Around 2014, Ave and I started camping, each time going a little farther into the woods. And in 2016, Ave proposed his most ambitious plan yet: hiking the entire one hundred miles of the Lone Star Trail through the Sam Houston National Forest. (See *Monster Hike*.) Of course, I agreed to partner up with him on this adventure. Unfortunately, when the time came in late 2016, I had to back out. It was devastating to break this news to him, but my work schedule simply wouldn't allow it.

Despite my absence, my friend had it in his mind to do it. And, of course, in typical Avrel fashion, he did it. Like a boss he did it. I was immensely proud of him, but I felt like I lost a chance to do something really epic. Because, frankly, over the years I've focused my efforts on raising boys, marathons, work, and managing the typical home projects. Doing something "epic" has never been at the forefront of my planning. However, Ave dreams big—it's part of what makes him special.

When Avrel suffered a stroke in 2018, leaving him significantly paralyzed on his right side, I believed our epic adventures were over. It was a very sobering and sad realization. But, once again, I forgot that Ave

AFTERWORD

dreams big. Just twelve months later, in January 2019, we were back out in the Sam Houston National Forest for our annual New Year's campout. A mile-long hike took about two hours, but we did it. It gave me hope.

Throughout 2019, Avrel kept working at his rehab and learning how to live with his limitations. Notice how I said "live"—not manage or cope. Ave isn't one to just manage and cope with a challenge. He hits everything head-on and will *not* let limitations limit him. He will figure out how to make it work. It's beautiful to witness. (See *With One Hand Tied behind My Brain*.)

In November 2019, Ave messaged me to meet up for breakfast on an upcoming Saturday morning. He offered to buy, and you now know the rest. However, I think it's worth noting another perspective while reading his account of our adventure. Why? Because, in *A Walk in the Woods*, we never really got to understand Katz's perspective—only Bill Bryson's rendition of Katz. There were two parties to this endeavor. One of them has the patience, talent, and skills to document all of it into a memoir. The other—well, you're reading it.

This adventure, or anything like it, was nothing that had ever crossed my mind as a desired undertaking; I stress *ever*. I lasted one campout in Boy Scouts almost forty years ago. Don't get me wrong—I love the outdoors—the coast, trails, mountains, forests. I love that running takes me outdoors. But I've also realized I love the indoors just as much. Each environment has its place, and I appreciate what each provides me. And Ave knows this. I'm still not sure why he picked me to join him. While Ave's goal was to soak in the experience and accomplish the goal of making it to the Gulf, *my* goal was to ensure my half-paralyzed friend and I came back home safely. As the event drew closer, my wife, Kelly, started to ask how I "felt" about all this. I think she could sense there was a tinge of dread and concern in my demeanor as it pertained to my preparation. While Avrel had done all of the painstaking planning and prep for the journey itself, my concern was ensuring we'd survive this

AFTERWORD

undertaking. For me, that meant a drybag to hold vital provisions: a 9mm, dry cigarettes, a charged cell phone, a power cell, and a LifeStraw. Ultimately, those five items were always kept near me. While this small list may seem dismissive to most, I felt these items were what would keep us alive and would allow me to function at a level required to stay alive if we found ourselves in an emergency.

The real test of will and determination revealed itself at the end of day one and, really, never let up until we hopped into Ave's pickup on day five. Almost five months after our adventure, the gravity of the responsibility I felt during this adventure still hits me from time to time. While Avrel and I were together on this journey, there were times I felt very alone as I contemplated what a rescue might mean. While this was a team effort, I believed any emergency primarily fell onto my shoulders. Not to say Avrel isn't capable, but the topography and remote sections of this river left us vulnerable to the surroundings.

We all deal with stress and conflict in our own way. Mine is to shut down all senses other than those required to survive. As day one ended, that instinct kicked in and lasted until we loaded the kayak into the pickup on day five. Not until we sat in the cab of the truck and the A/C hit my face did I realize that I could let that sense of impending doom subside. Later that same evening, I realized that my body and mind had been in a fight-or-flight mode for as many hours as we traveled miles on the water. That extracts a price on the body and spirit.

I'm probably too old to fundamentally change my perspective on things, but I will always be thankful to have this experience as a reflection point when I find myself in a similar environment. I now know what to expect from myself, and it will allow me to approach and handle the next event with a sense of knowledge and experience versus a sense of doom. I owe my friend a huge thank you for unknowingly giving me a new level of self-awareness. I thank my friend for allowing me to share my perspective (assuming this makes it into the book).

AFTERWORD

But I would be remiss without reminding you that every single effort, event, situation, and challenge we encountered meant that Avrel faced it with only one side of his body. I'm not enough of a wordsmith to explain what this means. But, if you're holding this book in both hands while enjoying a cup of coffee, sit on your right hand and do the same thing. Now, take that same limitation and put your ass in a kayak and travel eighty-six miles on an untamed river.

For me, this is one of the highlights of my lifetime—and I've had many. I will always be grateful for the challenge, the memories, the people met along the way, the lessons learned, and the personal insights I uncovered. Thank you to my wife, Kelly, and my boys for your willingness to support this endeavor. I love you all more than you'll ever really understand. Thank you to Erren for saving our asses on day two. Thank you to all the people we met along the way. Your generosity was true and unfiltered. Frankly, I'm still amazed at how our paths crossed in such a timely manner. And thank you to Kirstin for being there when we needed you. It's hard to put into words how much your arrival meant to us in the end.

To my friend Avrel—what you did out there still amazes me. What you accomplish every day amazes me. To see your sheer will and determination is inspiring, even more so when I look back on what I saw you push yourself to do, in some cases, to complete a task that most of us take for granted on a daily basis. Love you, you crazy sumbitch. *Ánda!*

—**WADE WALKER,**
October 2020

ACKNOWLEDGMENTS

Wade Walker, for making it all possible by his willingness, steadfastness, and perseverance. My wife, Kirstin, for enduring the kayak in the front room and the kayak in the front yard, for the shuttle service to Webberville, and to Bastrop, and to George West, and to Corpus, and the supportive attitude. David McLeod, for the leather foot strap, for saving the kayak, and for the illustrations. My brother Erren, for the Lake Corpus Christi portage, the cold water, and the cover photography. My mother, Jan, for the early feedback on the manuscript. And TCU Press for the platform to tell my story.

ABOUT THE AUTHOR

Photo by Kristin Seale

AVREL SEALE is the author of ten books, including memoir, humor, history, religion, and unsolved mystery. Much of his career has been at the University of Texas at Austin, as editor of its alumni magazine, speechwriter for its president, and a writer for its news, marketing, and development offices. He and his wife, Kirstin, have three sons.

www.ingramcontent.com/pod-product-compliance
Lightning Source LLC
Chambersburg PA
CBHW031456160426
43195CB00010BB/998